SHORT NATURE WALKS
CONNECTICUT

"Using this guide, you and your family can enjoy a few hours in the woods any season of the year and leave civilization behind."

—Woodall's *CamperWays* newsletter

"Complete information on trails and other hiking areas throughout the state."

—*The Day* (New London, Conn.)

Help Us Keep This Guide Up to Date

Every effort has been made by the editors to make this guide as accurate and useful as possible. However, many things can change after a guide is published—trails are rerouted, phone numbers change, facilities come under new management, and so on.

We would love to hear from you concerning your experiences with this guide and how you feel it could be improved and kept up to date. While we may not be able to respond to all comments and suggestions, we'll take them to heart and we'll also make certain to share them with the author. Please send your comments and suggestions to the following address:

The Globe Pequot Press
Reader Response/Editorial Department
P.O. Box 480
Guilford, CT 06437

Or you may e-mail us at:
editorial@globe-pequot.com

Thanks for your input, and happy travels!

A FALCON GUIDE®

SHORT NATURE WALKS
CONNECTICUT

Seventh Edition

by EUGENE KEYARTS

revised and updated by CINDI DALE PIETRZYK

FALCON®

GUILFORD, CONNECTICUT
HELENA, MONTANA

AN IMPRINT OF THE GLOBE PEQUOT PRESS

To all the volunteers out there who work tirelessly
on our state's trails and in our state parks and forests
to keep them beautiful and safe—you don't have to do it,
and we appreciate it. Thanks.

Acknowledgments

The community of hikers is one of cooperation, education, and die-hard fans. I'd like to thank the scores of people who helped with this book. These include the many trail managers who reviewed text and maps, rewrote walks, redrew maps, and patiently explained changes to me. To those who received endless e-mail messages from me begging for help at the last minute—thanks. I'd also like to thank these individuals for their help: Bill Schumacher, Bob Mocarsky, Chuck Keating, Clyde Brooks, Dane Millette, Dean Birdsall, Dick Sweetnam, Ed Merry, Gerald Smith, Kent Heidenis, Mike Broderick, Mike Stanley, Robert Schofff, the folks at Old New-Gate Prison and Gillette Castle, and Al Levere and Robert Reynolds, Connecticut Department of Environmental Protection.

I can't forget to thank Ann Colsen for pointing me in the right direction and getting me started.

My appreciation goes to Chris and Jesse Brunson, previous editors of this book—look for their bits of Connecticut lore and helpful hints throughout the write-ups.

I'd like to recognize Eugene Keyarts—original author of *Short Nature Walks Connecticut*. He started it all, and we all endeavor to continue a book of which he would be proud.

I wholeheartedly thank Bruce Morton and Pat Young and family for their many hours of hiking and great map input!

My gratitude goes to my husband, Stephen, for the many hours of babysitting and multiple vacation days taken to allow me the time to finish this book. Also, thanks for the weekend hikes with our daughters—time I'll always treasure.

And lastly, I couldn't have completed this book without the help of my fellow hiker and brother-in-law, Bill Bensenhaver. For driving endless miles, hiking even more, editing write-ups, creating maps, and patiently reviewing everything—a heartfelt thank you.

Contents

Middlesex County

New Haven County

Fairfield County

Litchfield County

Preface

I have something to confess. When I decided to update this book, I was not a hiker. I wasn't even a nature enthusiast. I started with a love for this book and a belief that there were adventures to be had. I have something else to confess. I'm hooked. I knew Connecticut was a beautiful, diverse state. I even knew there were a lot of places I hadn't seen after living here almost my entire life. I didn't know it was this beautiful, and I didn't know there were so many places left unchanged by development, commercialism, humans.

You've got to get out there, discover what I did. There is nothing that compares to being in the middle of the woods and hearing no cars, seeing no houses, or even imagining that you're the only one on Earth.

The walks in this book are not difficult, for the most part. They're not very long, for the most part. They are beautiful and worth the effort, every one of them.

There's a lot of ground to cover so stop reading and get out on the trails. Start with this book and then you, too, will be hooked. I promise.

—*Cindi D. Pietrzyk*
Editor, seventh edition

Introduction

The walks in this book only begin to touch on the hiking trails in Connecticut. The Connecticut Forest and Park's Blue-Blazed Hiking Trail System alone covers more than 700 miles of trails—700 miles!

The walks described in this book are not for the hard-core hiker, although they are not without challenges. Some take you to mountain summits; some take you to the very edges of sheer cliffs. Others take you along miles of shoreline, while still others take you to Indian caves, war encampments, an old prison, a castle, even to the land of the dinosaurs!

The walks are arranged by county starting in north central Connecticut (Hartford County) and going in a clockwise direction. I've attempted to arrange the walks within the counties along a logical driving route in case you want to do more than one in a day. Sometimes, however, the driving distances can be a bit long between starting points.

Please obtain and use a Connecticut state map when attempting to locate trailheads. My directions are accurate, but my maps are for reference only.

What to Wear and Bring

- Sturdy shoes, preferably boots that support and protect ankles with a cleated composition sole. (Leather soles are apt to become slippery.) Don't break in a pair of new footwear on a walk—your feet will be grateful. Equip children with good shoes or boots as well; their comfort will make your walk more enjoyable.

- Two pairs of socks to cushion the feet and absorb excessive perspiration. If you cannot tolerate wool against your skin, wear a pair of light cotton or silk socks underneath a pair of wool socks.

- Insect repellent (deer flies can be irritating as can the mosquitoes you'll encounter in the warmer months), tissues, a basic first-aid kit, and sunglasses. A light knapsack in which to carry these items, as well as lunch and other gear, is especially useful as it leaves your hands free.

- Comfortable clothing. Loose-fitting pants are better than shorts; a lightweight sweater or flannel shirt gives extra warmth; a windbreaker or parka provides protection against wind and rain. A wide-brimmed hat has several advantages: It protects the eyes from glaring sun; it keeps rain or snow off neck and face; and it gives slightly more protection from insects.

- Water. In addition to water, you might find a thermos filled with hot or cold (nonalcoholic) liquid a nice trail treat. Take a suitable lunch, depending on how much time you plan to spend on the trail. Food may vary from sandwiches to fruit and raisins. There's nothing quite like fresh air to whet an appetite and add flavor to a simple meal.

- Binoculars or a camera. But be careful not to overload yourself with too much gear. A map and compass may not be absolutely essential but are recommended—as is a detailed topographical map. Sometimes a good way to get familiar with a trail is to go on a guided hike first. Losing your way is not funny and can be dangerous if you get hurt or the weather turns severe. Also, never start a walk at dusk.

- A field guide to flowers, trees, birds, rocks, or other subjects, depending on your particular interests. These can add to the enjoyment and educational value of any walk.

Always, always pack out what you've packed in. Many of the miles of trails are on private property, and if we don't take care of the area, landowners will close their property and many trails could be lost. We need to preserve our natural lands for future generations to enjoy; let's not leave our trash, too.

Beware of Hunters

If you live in a suburban area, hunting is something of which you may not even be aware; however, throughout much of the state, hunting is a regular activity, especially in autumn. Don't assume where you hike is off-limits. If you are alert and use your common sense, you can still take pleasant walks during this season, but be sure to wear bright clothing—blaze orange is best.

Walkers should be aware that peak hunting season for small game and deer lasts from the third Saturday in October through December, especially in the early morning hours. No Sunday hunting is allowed in the state, except at registered private shooting preserves. Hunting does not occur in most state parks and incidents involving non-hunters are extremely rare, but stay alert.

Caution. . .

When walking in the woods, grassland, or marshland, take precautions against ticks, especially the deer tick, *Ixodes dammini*. The bite of some ticks transmits a spirochete bacterium, which may cause Lyme disease. Early symptoms of Lyme disease are a rash or red patch on the skin, muscle ache, fever, chills, and fatigue.

To prevent tick bites, wear your shirt tucked into long pants with pant cuffs tucked into socks. White or light-colored clothing makes it easier to spot ticks. Insect repellents may be useful. Brush off clothing and pets when you return home. Undress and check for ticks: They usually crawl about for several hours before burrowing into your skin. Be vigilant—check leg and arm creases and heads and necks especially thoroughly.

Remove any ticks you find with tweezers (saving the tick in a jar for future reference); then wash the area and your hands with soap and water. If you develop symptoms of Lyme disease, consult a physician immediately.

Also be aware that rattlesnake sightings have occasionally been reported, particularly in the Meshomasic Forest and near rock exposures and traprock cliffs. Use common sense: Snakes like to bask in the sun's warmth—often on the same rock cliffs you want to walk across. Hikers should always wear sturdy shoes (those that protect ankles) and be alert to their surroundings.

You should also use precautions against mosquitoes, especially when walking in southeastern Connecticut during the summer. In recent years a few mosquitoes in this area have been found to carry a rare but serious disease called Eastern Equine Encephalitis (EEE).

To protect yourself from mosquito bites, you should avoid walking when the mosquitoes are most active—at dawn and at dusk—or wear long-sleeved shirts and long pants. Also use a mosquito repellent that contains DEET and follow the directions on the label.

Always check the weather before you leave. The last thing you want to do is get caught on a mountain in a thunderstorm, or get stuck on a trail in a cold rain or snow, or get caught in the heat without any water, or, well you get the idea.

It's always a good idea to leave word at home or some other place regarding your plans. And for safety's sake you should never walk alone. Besides, sharing with family and friends the pleasures of natural beauty and healthful activity will prove rewarding.

Lastly, don't overdo it while out walking; remember to turn back before tiring.

Trail Information

Trails along the Connecticut Blue-Blazed Hiking Trail System are marked with blue blazes. You'll find these mostly on trees but also on rocks and anything else that is semipermanent in the area. Be sure to check often that you are following these blue blazes so you don't accidentally stray off the trail and become lost. The blazes will be single splashes of paint. If you see two splashes, one above the other and a little off to the left, it means the trail veers to the left. The same goes if the blaze on top is a little off to the right. Follow the trail to the right. If you see blazes one directly above the other, this means you have reached the trail terminus.

Trails within state parks and forests are often on their own color-coded system. Be sure to follow trails carefully.

After you have walked some or all of the trails listed in *Short Nature Walks Connecticut,* you may want some additional information about Connecticut trails.

For information about the Connecticut Blue Trails, contact:

Connecticut Forest and Park Association, 16 Meriden Road, Rockfall, CT 06481; (860) 346–2372; Web site: www.ctwoodlands.org.

For other information about state trails, nature centers, state parks, greenways, forests, and natural history, contact:

State of Connecticut Department of Environmental Protection, Parks, Forests and State Lands, 79 Elm Street, Hartford, CT 06106; Web site: www.dep.state.ct.us.

Other helpful sources:

Appalachian Trail Conference, P.O. Box 807, Harpers Ferry, WV 25425-0807; (304) 535–6331; fax: (304) 535–2667; Web site: www.atconf.org.

Appalachian Mountain Club, 5 Joy Street, Boston, MA 02108; (617) 523–0636; fax: (617) 523–0722; Web site: www.outdoors.org.

Topographical maps to supplement trail maps in this book can be obtained from the U.S. Geological Survey, Washington, DC 20242.

State topographical maps and publications about geology, botany, and more are available from the Department of Environmental Protection store located at 79 Elm Street, Hartford, Connecticut 06106.

Other helpful Web sites:

www.friendsctstateparks.net
www.falconoutdoors.com
www.globe-pequot.com

A Special Note: Before You Walk

Change is the rule of nature, but often her changes are slow, barely perceptible, and usually beneficial. Humans, in contrast, sometimes make drastic changes to solve immediate problems, only to create more harmful situations for the future.

Because of man-made changes—superhighways, crowded developments, and shopping complexes—we continue to destroy acres and acres of irreplaceable natural areas.

Because disruption and change are inevitable, we can only suggest that the user of this guide accept and comply with all trespass regulations. In many instances, however, a polite request of the property owner for permission to follow a trail over private land is usually granted.

Connecticut State Map

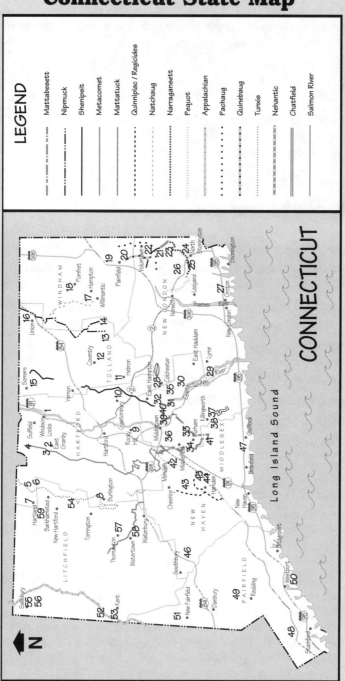

Connecticut Blue-Blazed Hiking Trail System

The main trails of the Connecticut Blue-Blazed Hiking Trail System have been given Native American names. The two major trails in southeastern Connecticut are named for the Narragansett and Pequot Indians, who lived in, hunted, and roamed the area. While walking these trails, be aware that you are following in the footsteps of these Native Americans.

Trails once crisscrossed the state in every direction. None, however, compared in importance for both Native American and colonist as the "Old Connecticut Path" and the "Shore Path." The first led west to the Hudson River from Hartford (called Suckiag by Native Americans) and east to Shawmut, now Boston. The latter shore path was more heavily traveled and of greater importance—it ran east from Manhattan to Shawmut and eventually was transformed into Route 1, also called the Boston Post Road.

Many of the older highways in the state follow paths originally made by the feet and travel of members of the seventeen tribal nations that shared the state prior to 1636. Not all trails have been converted to highways.

These are the blue-blazed trails referred to in this book. This is by no means an exhaustive list of the trails in the state, nor do our walks cover the entire trails.

Appalachian Trail— (*Note:* This is technically *not* a blue-blazed trail; we include it as a courtesy.) Springer Mountain in Georgia to Mount Katahdin in Maine; approximately 2,100 miles. Enters Connecticut at the New York state line in Sherman and leaves at Sages Ravine, just north of the Massachusetts state line in Salisbury.

Chatfield Trail—runs from Route 80 in Killingworth west of Chatfield Hollow State Park to River Road in Killingworth; 4.3 miles.

Mattabesett Trail—runs from Route 154 in Haddam to Route 15 in Meriden; bears the name that Native Americans gave to the area that's now Middletown. Has three divisions—eastern, central, and northern—that are connected by several miles of paved roads; 50-plus miles.

Mattatuck Trail—runs from Mad River Road in Wolcott to its junction with the Mohawk Trail in Cornwall; bears the name Native Americans gave to the area between Waterville and Naugatuck; 38 miles.

Metacomet Trail—runs approximately 54 miles in Connecticut; continues across Massachusetts to Mount Monadnock in New Hampshire. Metacomet was the name of an Indian who held dominion over this area during colonial days. It is alleged that he directed the burning of Simsbury from one of the summits on this trail.

Narragansett Trail—the Ledyard–North Stonington boundary line northeast to the Rhode Island border; 16 miles.

Natchaug Trail—Goodwin State Forest in Hampton and Westford; 19.2 miles.

Nehantic Trail—Green Falls Pond to Hopeville Pond State Park; 13 miles.

Nipmuck Trail—runs from Mansfield to Massachusetts border in Union; about 39 miles.

Pachaug Trail—Beach Pond on the Connecticut–Rhode Island state line west to Pachaug Pond in Griswold; approximately 30 miles.

Pequot Trail—runs from Ledyard to North Stonington, where it joins the Narragansett Trail in the town of North Stonington; 11 miles.

Quinebaug Trail—southern section in Voluntown, its northern half in Plainfield; 6.4 miles mostly on woodsy roads in the Pachaug State Forest.

Quinnipiac Trail—the oldest trail in Connecticut, started in 1929; runs from North Haven to Cheshire; 23 miles.

Salmon River Trail System—Colchester within Salmon River Watershed; 3 miles.

Shenipsit Trail—runs from East Hampton to Massachusetts state line with some breaks; 33 miles.

Tunxis Trail—consists of nineteen trails that run, with some breaks, from Southington to Massachusetts state line; 82 miles.

Windsor Locks Canal
Windsor Locks

Distance: 10 miles one way

Difficulty: Easy

This flat, paved trail takes you along a former tow path with the historic Windsor Locks Canal on one side and the Enfield Rapids and the Connecticut River on the other. The total path is almost 10 miles, but you can turn around at any point you wish, or you can park at either end and do the entire length.

The canal was built in the mid-1800s, and mules and horses were used to pull barges along the canal using this path. Today, anglers, bird-watchers, cyclists, and hikers take advantage of this now-paved trail to enjoy the beauty of the river and its surroundings. It's not uncommon to see Canada geese, mallard ducks, and blue heron gracing the skies. The waters are popular with anglers who come for some of the best shad fishing in New England.

The botanists in your group will appreciate the wildflowers that sprout all along the path. Watch out—poison ivy also makes its home here and sometimes reaches out over the pavement.

The path is maintained by the Connecticut Department of Environmental Protection and the state Department of Transportation and is open from spring through fall. In winter, the entrance is gated.

> **TRAIL TIPS**
>
> The path is popular with cyclists; keep an eye out for their passage and give them the right-of-way. Trail food and water may be purchased in Windsor Locks; be sure to bring lots of water with you on a hot day as the paved trail can really absorb the heat.

A Historical Perspective

The Windsor Locks Canal was built in the 1800s for transportation of material to Springfield, Massachusetts. Before that, items had to be off-loaded in Windsor then transported over land to Springfield because boats could not traverse the Enfield rapids. Today the canal is still used for water power.

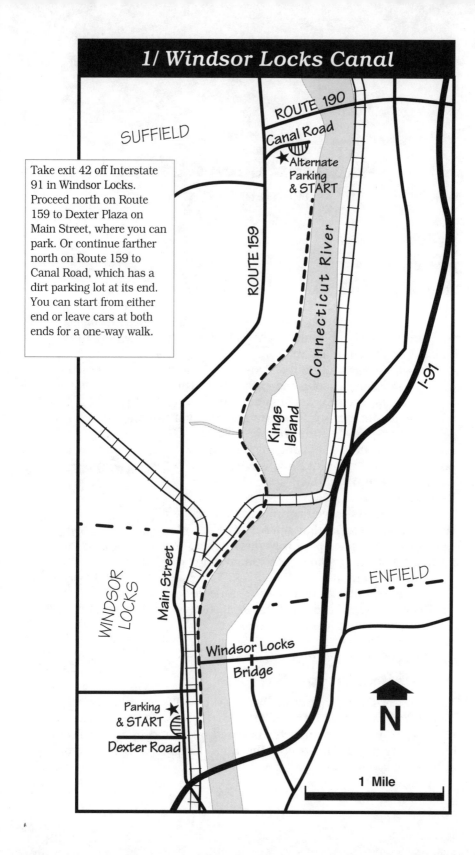

1/ Windsor Locks Canal

SUFFIELD

ROUTE 190

Canal Road

★ Alternate
Parking
& START

Take exit 42 off Interstate 91 in Windsor Locks. Proceed north on Route 159 to Dexter Plaza on Main Street, where you can park. Or continue farther north on Route 159 to Canal Road, which has a dirt parking lot at its end. You can start from either end or leave cars at both ends for a one-way walk.

ROUTE 159

Connecticut River

Kings Island

I-91

ENFIELD

WINDSOR LOCKS

Main Street

Windsor Locks
Bridge

N

Parking
& START ★

Dexter Road

1 Mile

Old New-Gate Wildlife Trail
East Granby

Distance: 0.8 mile round-trip

Difficulty: Easy

This wonderful walk is suitable for all ages and can be combined with a visit to the historic Old New-Gate Prison for a memorable day trip.

The walk starts from the prison parking lot, near a map board that gives details about the walk.

The trail is a 0.8-mile walk through woods and wetlands. It is maintained by the Connecticut Department of Environmental Protection's Wildlife Division and is operated in cooperation with the Connecticut Historical Commission, which oversees the prison. The trail offers a fascinating look into wildlife habitat management practices, old field growth, and ways in which plantings can attract birds. The path leads through woods to the edge of a field, bends along the old field area, and winds past Newgate Pond. A detailed brochure about the vegetation and wildlife is sometimes available from a map board at the start of the walk or from the visitors' center, when it is open. There are some portions where you cross wooden footbridges directly through wetlands. Wear long pants as poison ivy can get the better of the trail in some spots.

When you end your walk, head to the prison to explore the underground mines and historic ruins. A three-dimensional relief map tablet, located on the park grounds, depicts the major mountains and peaks of the Farmington Valley, of which you have breathtaking views.

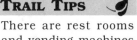

TRAIL TIPS

There are rest rooms and vending machines at the visitors' center. Admission is charged to the prison, but access to the grounds and nature walk is free. Currently open mid-May through mid-October. The parking lot is gated off-season and closed after 4:30 P.M. in season. Parking along the road is risky.

A Historical Perspective

Old New-Gate Prison, with crumbling ruins above ground and the tunnels of the mine below, is fascinating. The prison is state property

Reach the historic site from either Route 190 in Suffield or Route 20 in East Granby. The shortest approach is from Route 20 on the south. To reach this point follow the most convenient route to the intersection of Routes 20 and 187 in East Granby. Follow Route 20 west 0.6 mile to Newgate Road, on the right. Travel north on Newgate Road until you reach the site; parking is on the left, just past the signs.

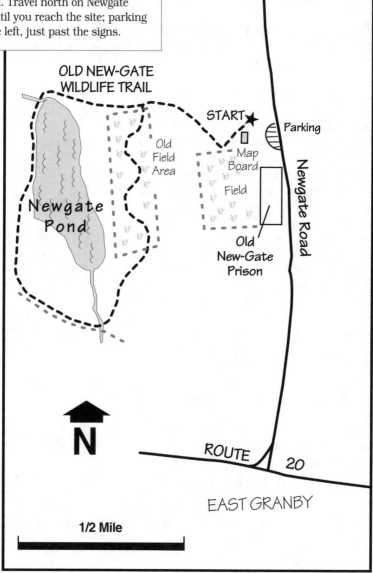

SUFFIELD

OLD NEW-GATE
WILDLIFE TRAIL

START ★   Parking

Old
Field
Area

Map
Board

Field

Newgate
Pond

Old
New-Gate
Prison

Newgate Road

N

ROUTE 20

EAST GRANBY

1/2 Mile

and is open to the public. Its history began in 1705, when it was known as Copper Hill and the first mining probe for copper was started. In 1707 a group of land proprietors of Simsbury formed the first company to work the mines.

In 1773 the Colony of Connecticut first used the tunnels and caverns 30 feet below the surface as a permanent prison. It was during the American Revolution that the title of the prison was changed to New-Gate after Newgate Prison of London, England. In 1781 Congress made New-Gate of Connecticut a government jail for prisoners of war. During its fifty-four years as a prison, many British, Tory, and state prisoners were kept in the dank, dark dungeons. As many as forty prisoners at one time were confined in the rock-hewn holes, and they were compelled to work in the mine and workshops. In the 1820s female prisoners were sent to New-Gate, but they were kept in cells above ground.

After 1827, when Wethersfield was made a state prison site, Old New-Gate Prison was abandoned.

Peak Mountain
East Granby

Distance: 3 miles round-trip with option for more

Difficulty: Moderate

This hike takes you up Peak Mountain to the highest point on the Metacomet Trail between Tariffville and the Massachusetts state line. The trail is rocky in spots, but it's not too tiring if you pace it. There are good vistas and it is a popular spot for viewing autumn foliage. Follow the trail north up a very steep wooded slope. Numerous unmarked trails join up with the blue-blazed hiking trail from the parking area. Stone outcrops poke through the leaf litter and underbrush. The trail continues north on the crest of the ridge, with fine views to the west. Peak Mountain is reached 1 mile from Route 20; the trail leads north along the crest of Peak Mountain through hardwood forest to Turkey Hills Lookout, at approximately 1.5 miles from the starting point. You may wish to rest and picnic here while enjoying the distant views. You are now 672 feet above sea level.

TRAIL TIPS

No facilities are available. Parking is along trail entrance and can get crowded. Bring along trail food or stop at nearby convenience store in East Granby for snacks.

Should you desire to go farther, continue on the blazed trail, which goes north to Manituck Lookout (Walk 4) and then into Massachusetts, or retrace your steps and return from any point you decide.

There is an extra bonus that may be combined with this walk to Peak Mountain. This section of the Metacomet Trail parallels Newgate Road, on which Old New-Gate Prison is located. (On a clear day the prison can be seen from the lookout.) It is only 1.2 miles north from Route 20 to the crumbling remains of what was once a busy copper mine and later a state prison and a federal jail. If you're not too tired, there are nature trails to be explored there as well (Walk 2).

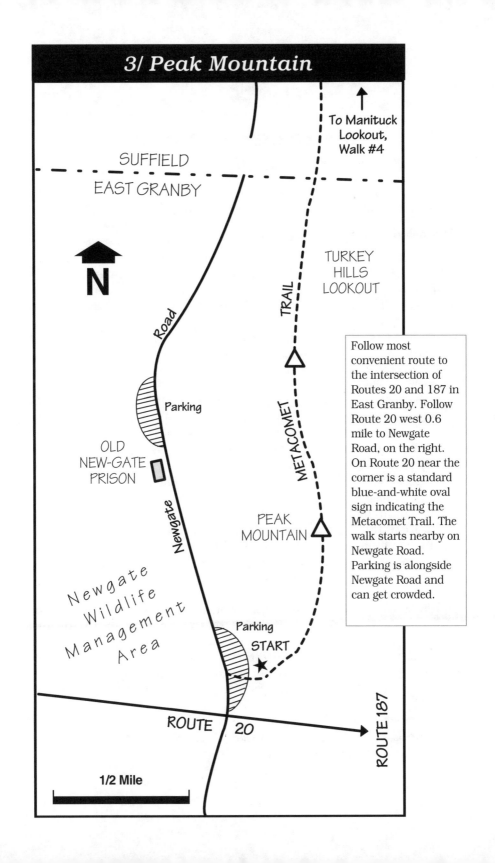

3/ Peak Mountain

SUFFIELD

EAST GRANBY

To Manituck
Lookout,
Walk #4

N

TURKEY
HILLS
LOOKOUT

Road

TRAIL

Parking

METACOMET

OLD
NEW-GATE
PRISON

PEAK
MOUNTAIN

Newgate

Newgate
Wildlife
Management
Area

Parking
START

Follow most convenient route to the intersection of Routes 20 and 187 in East Granby. Follow Route 20 west 0.6 mile to Newgate Road, on the right. On Route 20 near the corner is a standard blue-and-white oval sign indicating the Metacomet Trail. The walk starts nearby on Newgate Road. Parking is alongside Newgate Road and can get crowded.

ROUTE 20

ROUTE 187

1/2 Mile

Manituck Lookout
Suffield

Distance: 2 miles one way with option for more

Difficulty: Moderate, some steep climbs

This steady uphill walk along the Metacomet Trail leads you to mountain outlooks atop traprock ridges with views of the valley and far-flung mountains. Vantage points along the trail are columnlike traprock with rock scree below. The columnar joints appear to have been raked by fingers. In early spring many woodland wildflowers, including lady slippers, blanket the area. In late spring wild columbine appears on sunny rock outcrops along the ridge top. Scenery is spectacular with no particular sights other than rolling mountains and the sprawling valley.

The walk begins with several switchbacks as the trail ascends to a woods road. At about 0.5 mile watch for an old stone chimney and bench reminiscent of a past cabin off to the left (east). They're about 100 feet off the trail, and if leaf cover isn't too dense, they should be pretty easy to spot. Shortly after that, the trail leaves the woods road and heads right. (Follow the sign.) At about 1 mile watch for a sign THE GEORGE A. HARMON WOODLOT. At this point you have your options of what you can do.

Option 1: Turn opposite the George Harmon sign and look for a sign reading DEER RUN. You can follow this trail downridge to the left approximately 0.5 mile to see the town's Sunrise Park. Be warned, however, that this is a hike down several hundred feet in altitude, to a level lower than the trailhead. Obviously the hike back is work, a little steeper and longer than the climb at the trailhead but more moderate than difficult. Sunrise Park is about 130 acres of woodland containing several easy trails including one around 20-acre Whites Pond. It's a nice place to picnic with some picnic tables as well as an outhouse.

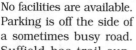

TRAIL TIPS

No facilities are available. Parking is off the side of a sometimes busy road. Suffield has trail supplies and food offerings.

Option 2: Follow the Metacomet Trail along the ridge, or you could follow the trail uphill until it reaches Manituck Lookout, where you

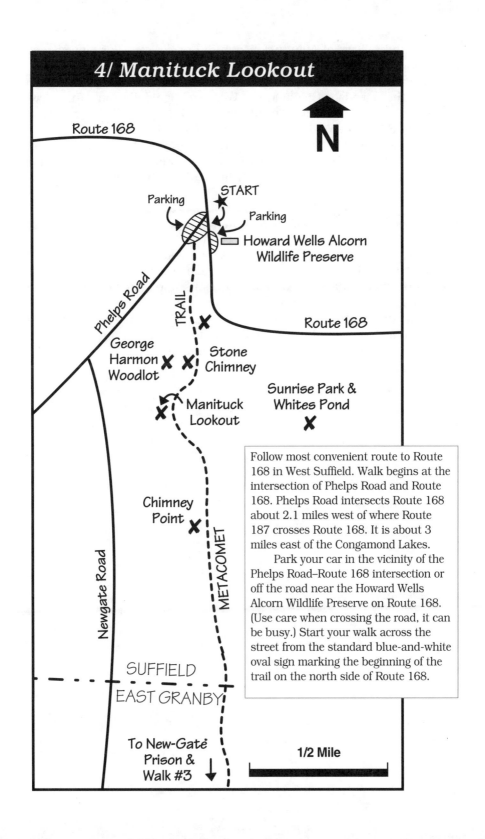

4/ Manituck Lookout

N

Route 168

Parking

START

Parking

Howard Wells Alcorn
Wildlife Preserve

Phelps Road

TRAIL

Route 168

George
Harmon
Woodlot

Stone
Chimney

Sunrise Park &
Whites Pond

Manituck
Lookout

Chimney
Point

METACOMET

Newgate Road

SUFFIELD

EAST GRANBY

To New-Gate
Prison &
Walk #3

1/2 Mile

Follow most convenient route to Route
168 in West Suffield. Walk begins at the
intersection of Phelps Road and Route
168. Phelps Road intersects Route 168
about 2.1 miles west of where Route
187 crosses Route 168. It is about 3
miles east of the Congamond Lakes.

Park your car in the vicinity of the
Phelps Road–Route 168 intersection or
off the road near the Howard Wells
Alcorn Wildlife Preserve on Route 168.
(Use care when crossing the road, it can
be busy.) Start your walk across the
street from the standard blue-and-white
oval sign marking the beginning of the
trail on the north side of Route 168.

can take in views of Manituck Mountain, a forested flat-topped rock mass to the west that is shaped like a pie. Walk for another 0.5 mile and you come to a traprock crag known as Chimney Point, from where the Barndoor Hills and the Western Highlands come into view. Once you've covered 2 miles, you'll have reached the East Granby–Suffield boundary marker and another lookout.

If you're getting tired or have had enough nature for one day, you can retrace your steps back to your car at Phelps Road. Or you may decide to follow the self-guiding trail south a little farther before returning to the starting point.

A Historical Perspective

Native Americans who lived in the central Connecticut Valley named this northernmost ridge in the state Amantuck, meaning "to see in the distance." It is said that Metacomet, a.k.a. King Philip (1639–1676), used the high ridges as strategic outlooks and that he oversaw the burning of Simsbury from the heights of Talcott Mountain. Just food for thought as you do your own exploring. Today, the Metacomet Trail (yes, named after him) traverses this mountain range, following much of the same ground as the Native Americans did.

Roberts Brook

Hartland

Distance: 3.4 miles one way, 4.7 miles with second car

Difficulty: Easy, some climbs

This hike along the northern region of the Tunxis Trail takes you through peaceful woods along a winding trail past Barkhamsted Reservoir and fields. It is suitable for most abilities and ages, with some inclines.

This walk starts on the left south side of Old Route 20 (Walnut Hill Road) where the blue-blazed Tunxis Trail crosses the road. The trail heads south and ascends immediately to a crest before it dips and rises over several hills and shortly reaches a barbed wire fence on the west, which it clings to for some of the way. Use care when following this trail; there are deceptive paths and woods roads that tend to lead one astray. Be sure to have a blue blaze in view before advancing too far.

Roberts Brook is reached at approximately 2.4 miles. The trail continues south for about 1 mile to Pine Mountain Road and the north base of Pine Mountain. You may return to your car after reaching Roberts Brook or extend your walk by 0.5 mile or so going on to Pine Mountain for a fine view of Springfield, Massachusetts, before returning to your car via the same path.

> **TRAIL TIPS**
>
> No facilities are available. Parking is along an unused road. Bring refreshments, as there are no food stops in the immediate area.

For this walk, you also have the option of parking a second car at the beginning of Pine Mountain Road at Route 179. You'd have to hike 0.75 mile down Pine Mountain Road from the blue-blazed hiking trail to your car.

Walk 6, Pine Mountain, is a continuation of this walk, and Walk 7, Tunxis State Forest, offers options in the opposite direction.

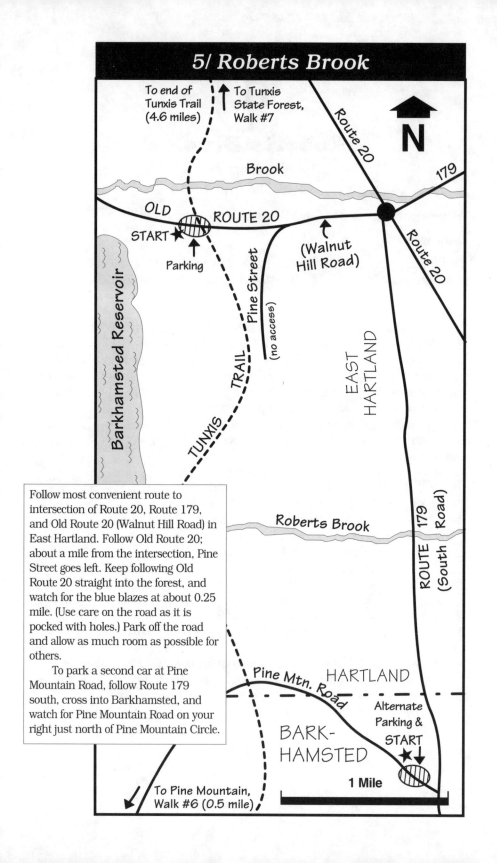

5/ Roberts Brook

To end of
Tunxis Trail
(4.6 miles)

To Tunxis
State Forest,
Walk #7

Route 20

N

179

Brook

OLD ROUTE 20

Route 20

START

Parking

Pine Street

(Walnut
Hill Road)

(no access)

Barkhamsted Reservoir

EAST
HARTLAND

TUNXIS TRAIL

Roberts Brook

ROUTE 179
(South Road)

Follow most convenient route to intersection of Route 20, Route 179, and Old Route 20 (Walnut Hill Road) in East Hartland. Follow Old Route 20; about a mile from the intersection, Pine Street goes left. Keep following Old Route 20 straight into the forest, and watch for the blue blazes at about 0.25 mile. (Use care on the road as it is pocked with holes.) Park off the road and allow as much room as possible for others.

To park a second car at Pine Mountain Road, follow Route 179 south, cross into Barkhamsted, and watch for Pine Mountain Road on your right just north of Pine Mountain Circle.

Pine Mtn. Road

HARTLAND

BARK-
HAMSTED

Alternate
Parking &
START

1 Mile

To Pine Mountain,
Walk #6 (0.5 mile)

6

Pine Mountain

Barkhamsted

Distance: 1.25 miles one way to summit, 3.5 miles loop back to car

Difficulty: Easy

Reaching the summit will reward you with a spectacular vista. From your parking spot, follow gravel Pine Mountain Road 0.75 mile to where the blue-blazed Tunxis Trail intersects. Turn left onto the Tunxis Trail and follow for 0.5 mile as the trail ascends the summit of Pine Mountain (1,391 feet). From here you have great views of East Hartland; Springfield, Massachusetts; and Bradley International Airport.

You can return to your car via the same route, or you can continue down the south face of Pine Mountain approximately 0.75 mile to Pine Mountain Road. Turn right and follow Pine Mountain Road approximately 1.5 miles to your car.

THE MIGHTY OAK

Connecticut's official state tree is the white oak. Botanists have given this tree the Latin name *Quercus alba*, meaning white oak, and classify it as a member of the Fagaceae (beech) family.

The white oak is an important timber tree, useful and valuable. Its tough, close-grained, durable wood has many uses in general construction, shipbuilding, furniture-making, cooperage, flooring, and so on. The tree's natural range is practically all of the eastern half of the United States. The average white oak attains a height of 80 to 100 feet and a diameter of 2 to 3 feet. It is one of the easiest of oaks to identify because of its distinctive light ashy-gray bark. The full-grown leaves are bright green above and much lighter below, 5 to 9 inches long and 2 to 3 inches broad, with seven or nine deeply cut, fingerlike lobes. The white oak's fruit is an acorn, which matures in one year; some oaks require two years to produce fruit. The white oak acorn grows to ¾ inch to 1 inch in length, is light brown in color, and is topped with a warty cap.

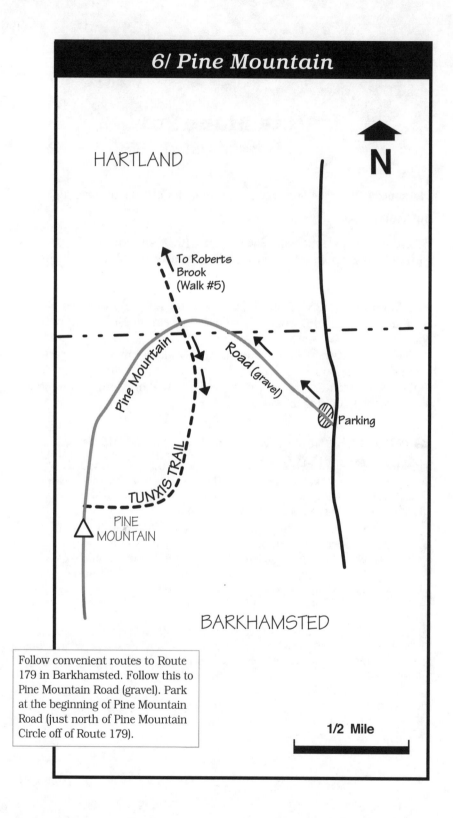

6/ Pine Mountain

HARTLAND

N

To Roberts
Brook
(Walk #5)

Pine Mountain

Road (gravel)

Parking

TUNXIS TRAIL

△ PINE
MOUNTAIN

BARKHAMSTED

Follow convenient routes to Route
179 in Barkhamsted. Follow this to
Pine Mountain Road (gravel). Park
at the beginning of Pine Mountain
Road (just north of Pine Mountain
Circle off of Route 179).

1/2 Mile

Tunxis State Forest
Hartland

Distance: 2 miles one way

Difficulty: Moderate, some climbs

This walk can be wet and steep in areas, but it is very remote and beautiful. While not suitable for small children or those not up to the strenuous parts, this is a blissful walk through some quiet woods over a cobbled stream with small waterfalls, through rolling meadows, and along stone walls.

You have the option of parking a car at both ends of this walk (one on Old Route 20 [Walnut Hill Road] and one on Route 20) or retracing your steps to either starting point.

The trailhead is off the right (north) side of Walnut Hill Road. (For walks heading the other direction, see Walks 5 and 6.) Follow the blue blazes as the trail leaves the road and soon crosses a delightful brook. It continues a short distance before descending into a glade where another, livelier brook flows into the Barkhamsted Reservoir. After crossing the brook and exploring the small waterfalls and dark pools, continue on the trail as it winds past a logged area and ascends gradually to a dirt road (Ski Road or Balance Rock Road). Follow the road briefly, then walk the easy path through a meadow area to reach Route 20 at about 2 miles from the start. Watch carefully for the trail at this point; there are few trees to mark and blazes could be hard to spot.

To return from here, retrace your steps to the dirt road where the trail reenters woods to the left or south. The dirt road was at one time the approach to a ski slope, once popular but now abandoned. The road is now used only as a part of an occasional cross-country ski run and as an approach to a cabin at the western end.

The state-owned log cabin (reserved exclusively for use by Boy Scout troops) is at the dead end of the dirt road about 0.25 mile west of the blue-blazed trail crossing. Although off the main part of the trail, a side trip will prove to be an extra bonus as

TRAIL TIPS

No facilities are available. Parking is in a pull-off on an unused road. Bring along trail treats, as there aren't any stores nearby.

MASSACHUSETTS

CONNECTICUT

N

TUNXIS

STATE

FOREST

Take most convenient route to the intersection of Route 20 (alternate parking), Route 179, and Old Route 20 (Walnut Hill Road) in East Hartland. Follow Old Route 20 straight into the forest (about 1 mile beyond the intersection with Pine Street on the left). Use care as the old paved road is now pocked with holes. Park off the road, leaving as much room as possible for others. The trail starts off the right (north) side of the road.

Parking
Alternate   START

TRAIL

ROUTE 20

Balance   Rock Road
(dirt)

Cabin

Brook

Waterfalls

TUNXIS

ROUTE 20

Brook

179

South Road

START   OLD ROUTE 20

Walnut Hill Road

Parking

EAST HARTLAND

ROUTE

1/2 Mile

To Walks
#5 & #6

it leads through an area fringed with ferns, accented with lichen-encrusted stone walls. (Lichen only grows where the air and water are clean; pollution kills it.)

This is an ideal spot to picnic and rest, enjoying the silence. Chipmunks abound in the area and love to perch on the stone walls, often scampering across the trail with their tails held straight up like rudders.

Returning from the cabin site, follow the road east to the blazed trail and then back to your car.

A Historical Perspective

The land now known as the Tunxis State Forest was probably never occupied or controlled by the Tunxis Indians, who were a subtribe of the Sicaogs. Grand Sachem Sequassen ruled both tribes. The Sicaogs claimed the area that is now Hartford and West Hartford, while the Tunxis tribe settled in the Farmington area, including much of the surrounding land.

The American Indian name for the Farmington River was Tunxis, which is an abbreviation for Tunxisepo, also Tunchseasapose. Both of these forms are short for Watunkshausepo, which means "fast-flowing and winding river." It is supposed to have described the sharp bend in the Farmington River where its flow changes abruptly from a southeasterly to a northerly course. It was quite natural that a tribe living in the Farmington River Valley became known as the Tunxis Indians.

What is now state forest was in all probability a part of the land in the northwest corner of Connecticut never permanently settled by any Native Americans. This was a sort of no-man's-land, constantly fought over by the Mohawks of New York and the Tunxis of Connecticut, both claiming the rich hunting ground as their own.

Mile of Ledges
Burlington

Distance: Approximately 3 miles for the loop

Difficulty: Challenging

This is a challenging, but rewarding loop walk. Said to be the roughest section of the Tunxis Trail, the Mile of Ledges is located in the south section of Burlington, quite near Bristol.

Once you park your car on Greer Road near Hill Street at the marsh, follow the blue-blazed hiking trail south over undulating terrain, ascending gradually to the Mile of Ledges.

At about 0.5 mile you will encounter one towering ledge after another. At about 1.1 miles you'll come upon a stone dam wall foundation with the center now torn down that once crossed the U-shaped valley. Once crossed over there are blocks and blocks of rock to clamber over and up.

The yellow-dot trail, which is marked by a blue blaze with a yellow dot in its center, is about 1.35 miles from the start. At the junction of the main blue-blazed Tunxis Trail with the yellow-dot trail, turn right (north) and follow the yellow-dot trail to historic Tory Den, about 0.2 mile. The den is located just off the side of the trail.

From Tory Den the yellow-dot trail continues north just over a mile to Greer Road Junction. Turn right, descend to Greer Road, and follow the road approximately 0.5 mile to your parked car.

Note: At the end of the yellow-dot trail, dogs should be leashed and under control to ensure the continued use of the trail over private land. The suburban neighborhood along the road makes for a pleasant stroll to return to your vehicle.

This area is rich in wildlife, rock ridges, second-growth forest, and almost meadow-like stretches. Although the round-trip is about 3 miles, plan to spend the day here, as climbing and navigating the rocky crags and exploring odd alleyways of stone will soak up hours. Along your journey, enjoy the chipmunks scurrying across fallen logs,

> **TRAIL TIPS**
>
> No facilities are available near the trail. Parking is limited at the trail's start; there are areas to park farther up Greer Road near the end of the trail loop. Nearby Bristol has food places aplenty.

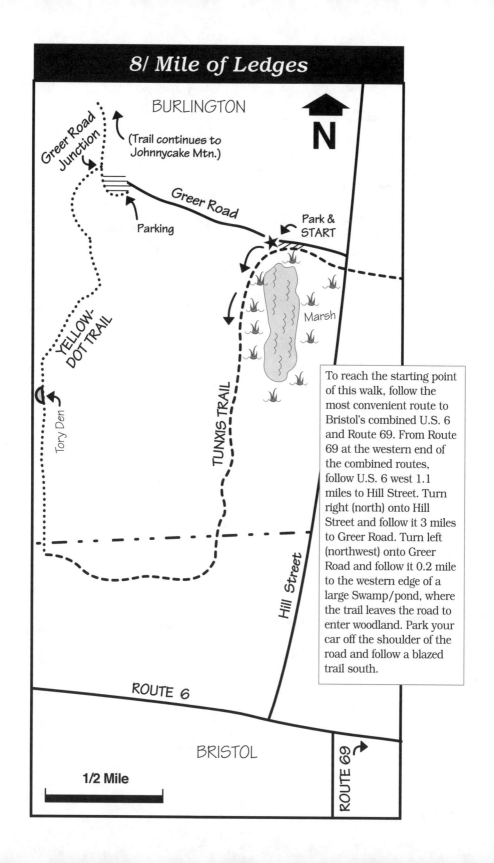

8/ Mile of Ledges

BURLINGTON

N

Greer Road Junction

(Trail continues to Johnnycake Mtn.)

Greer Road

Parking

Park & START

YELLOW-DOT TRAIL

Tory Den

TUNXIS TRAIL

Marsh

Hill Street

To reach the starting point of this walk, follow the most convenient route to Bristol's combined U.S. 6 and Route 69. From Route 69 at the western end of the combined routes, follow U.S. 6 west 1.1 miles to Hill Street. Turn right (north) onto Hill Street and follow it 3 miles to Greer Road. Turn left (northwest) onto Greer Road and follow it 0.2 mile to the western edge of a large Swamp/pond, where the trail leaves the road to enter woodland. Park your car off the shoulder of the road and follow a blazed trail south.

ROUTE 6

BRISTOL

ROUTE 69

1/2 Mile

pick out a boulder for a lunch spot, and savor the silence. Two snakes (both harmless) were spied on a recent walk along with three salamanders, a brightly mottled frog, and a tiny tree frog.

A Historical Perspective

The Tory Den is a historic landmark; it was used as a hideout during the Revolutionary War by the Chippens Hill Tories of the area when they were too hotly pressed by overzealous Patriots. Today the den, actually a tunnel beneath rock, continues to offer sanctuary, peace, and solitude to those who would flee momentarily the press of civilization. A nearby rock shelter (left of trail) with blackened-by-soot walls shows evidence of past campfires. The den was one of the stopovers reportedly used by the Old Leatherman in the 1800s (see Leatherman Cave, Walk 57).

Dinosaur State Park
Rocky Hill

Distance: 2.5 miles possible

Difficulty: Easy, some tricky terrain

This is a walk through Connecticut's own "Jurassic Park" that can be made any time during the year and that all ages can enjoy. Choose a circuitous loop or walk across a boardwalk, especially wonderful in the spring when frogs and new flowers may be seen. In summer, explore the theme gardens.

There are more than 200 species of plant families and trees that grow on the grounds of this unique state park. Along its 2.5 miles of nature trails, you will find a butterfly garden (especially fascinating in the summer), a bat house, and beautiful wildflower gardens. The trail is pretty easy (although not stroller or wheelchair accessible) as it meanders through woods, across swamp boardwalks, and along old orchards. There are a couple of steep climbs on the narrow trail and lots of exposed roots, so watch young children closely.

Varied natural history (birds, star-gazing, wildlife) walks are offered as well; check for schedules.

Dinosaur State Park boasts the largest concentration of tracks on a single layer of rock in North America. It is the largest enclosed and interpreted dinosaur trackway in North America.

The fossil imprints were discovered in 1966 during excavation for a building. Construction was halted and scientists called in. The remarkable site then became a ten-acre state park.

At the time of the dinosaurs, this area was part of a lake-plain with muddy conditions that were ideal for making the tracks. A traprock ridge and broken chunks of basaltic rock located in the park speak

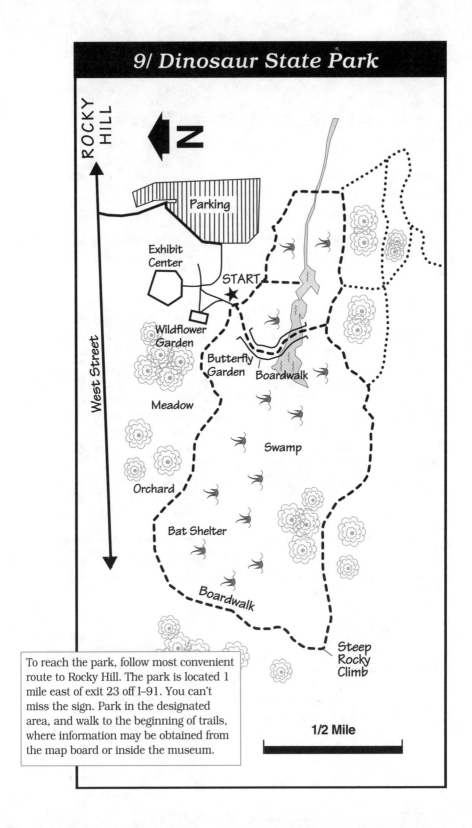

9/ Dinosaur State Park

ROCKY HILL

N

Parking

Exhibit Center

START

Wildflower Garden

Butterfly Garden

West Street

Boardwalk

Meadow

Swamp

Orchard

Bat Shelter

Boardwalk

Steep Rocky Climb

To reach the park, follow most convenient route to Rocky Hill. The park is located 1 mile east of exit 23 off I–91. You can't miss the sign. Park in the designated area, and walk to the beginning of trails, where information may be obtained from the map board or inside the museum.

1/2 Mile

of the hot lava that eventually covered the watery habitat of the dinosaurs.

Only a small portion of the trackway (although still awesome) is on display under the geodesic dome exhibit center; much of the fossilized imprints remain buried for protection.

Did You Know?

Did you know Connecticut has an official state fossil? (We didn't either.) But, it does—Eubrontes. Only its birdlike tracks can be seen at Dinosaur State Park; no skeletal remains of the animal have yet been discovered. Scientists believe Eubrontes was similar to the Dilphosaurus, a large carnivorous dinosaur in the Jurassic period.

10

Glacial Boulders
Glastonbury

Distance: Less than 3 miles one way, 5.5 miles for straight-through with Walk 11

Difficulty: Moderate

All of Connecticut was covered with a vast sheet of ice during the glacial period, and evidence of that is everywhere in the state. This walk takes you to an interesting deposit of glacial boulders on the Shenipsit Trail in the town of Glastonbury.

To reach the Shenipsit Trail from Birch Mountain Road, follow an access trail, the John Tom Hill Trail, marked with blue and red. Follow this access trail for about 0.5 mile as it passes under power lines, crosses a brook, and then ascends to its junction with the blue-blazed Shenipsit.

Many side paths crisscross the main Shenipsit trail; be sure to periodically check for blue blazes to ensure you are walking on the correct path. Mountain-bike enthusiasts frequent this section of the woods; keep alert for their passage.

Once on the blue-blazed Shenipsit Trail, follow it to the northeast and cross an old dirt road. The trail continues up some steep scrambles to Pine Ledge, with a fair view of Hartford, which is visible through the trees to the west (depending on leaf coverage). This is a fine area for lunch or a snack; be sure to pack up and take your leftovers with you when you leave. Leaving Pine Ledge, the trail continues north and crosses a junction with the blue-and-white blazed trail that will lead you to Gay City State Park in Hebron, which is 2.2 miles from where you are (see Walk 11).

> **TRAIL TIPS** 🍃
>
> There are no rest rooms. Parking is off a sometimes busy road. Nearby Glastonbury and Hebron are good places to pick up refreshments for the trail.

The Shenipsit keeps heading north and descends through a sag and open woods before climbing to the top of Garnet Ledge, about 1.7 miles from the start of the walk. The ledge was so named because it and many of the boulders are studded with tiny, pencil-tipped garnets (you have to look closely). Garnets are reddish in color. Minuscule

10/ Glacial Boulders

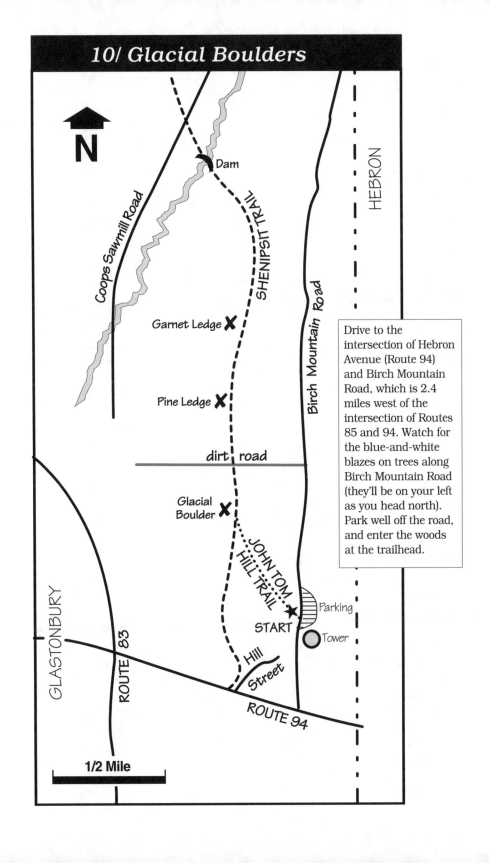

N

Coops Sawmill Road

Dam

SHENIPSIT TRAIL

HEBRON

Garnet Ledge ✗

Pine Ledge ✗

Birch Mountain Road

dirt road

Glacial Boulder ✗

JOHN TOM HILL TRAIL

★ Parking

START

Tower

GLASTONBURY

ROUTE 83

Hill Street

ROUTE 94

1/2 Mile

Drive to the intersection of Hebron Avenue (Route 94) and Birch Mountain Road, which is 2.4 miles west of the intersection of Routes 85 and 94. Watch for the blue-and-white blazes on trees along Birch Mountain Road (they'll be on your left as you head north). Park well off the road, and enter the woods at the trailhead.

loose stones that have washed out from the rock can be found in the sand.

Should you wish to go farther, you may follow the self-guiding trail northwest to an old dam, heading straight north, then west to Roaring Brook, before reaching Coops Sawmill Road, less than 3 miles from the start. You can then retrace your steps back to your car on Birch Mountain Road.

A Historical Perspective

It is estimated that these boulders were dumped in this area approximately 20,000 years ago. All of Connecticut was drastically changed by the work of the great glacier. Geologists guess that the ice at its peak was more than 1,000 feet thick on top of the New Haven area and that it exerted a pressure of 50,000 pounds per square foot on everything it passed over.

Its advance and retreat obliterated old land and rivers, creating new lands and bodies of water. Thanks to the work of the glacier, our state is blessed with a total of 1,026 lakes and 420 swamps.

As you walk this trail, you will become aware that, even though you appear to be on high ground, you are actually completely surrounded by much higher hills. Very likely the crags and rugged peaks of the surrounding mountains were bulldozed by the gigantic mass of ice, which then held the rough rocks in its grasp for centuries, grinding and shaping them into the forms in which we now see them. As the ice sheet melted, the captive mellowed stones were released many miles from their origin.

IN THE AREA

This walk could be combined with Walk 11 (Gay City) for a longer hike. Or, you could park one car on Birch Mountain Road and one car at Gay City State Park for a straight-through hike of about 5.5 miles.

Nature Along the Way

Along your journey note the scablike lichens that cling to the boulders. Called "time stains," these slow-growing life forms may be hundreds of years old. Recent rain or snow will freshen their appearance. Mountain laurel and wild blueberry shrubs are abundant along the path. The delicate blossom of the mountain laurel is Connecticut's state flower; the shrub blooms in the spring and is a relation of the garden rhododendron. Also note the sometimes thick veins of quartz that are visible in the twisted outcroppings of ancient rock. They resemble toothpaste that has been squeezed into rock crevices.

Bird life is also abundant along this trail. Various types of hawks frequent the updrafts east of Pine Ledge and can be seen circling on air currents.

Gay City State Park
Hebron

Distance: 10 miles of walking trails in the park, white trail is 2.5 miles

Difficulty: Moderate, some steep climbs

Gay City is a real live ghost town, a community that now exists only in the pages of local history. Once known as Factory Hollow, the name Gay City was stipulated by owners when they turned the land over to the state for use as a state park. Hiking trails throughout the park are well marked and offer the opportunity for a day-long hike or a relaxing afternoon ramble.

Once you park, check to see if a ranger is on duty; if one is, ask for a free map showing locations of all the trails and other features of the area. Maps may also be picked up at the trail display board located by the parking lot near Route 85 (this lot is used in winter when the park is gated to traffic).

A pleasant walk for all abilities is the white-blazed trail, which heads through the park and comes down around the pond, parallels the Blackledge River for a bit, and then passes the old mill ruins before taking you back to your car.

> **TRAIL TIPS**
>
> Outhouses are located throughout the park, as are picnic areas. Glastonbury and Hebron are a short drive away for food and refreshments. In summer, a small beach and swimming area are open. Winter-fall-spring parking is at the lot near Route 85. Cross-country skiing is popular in the park. *Note:* Stay alert for passage of equestrians and their mounts on park trails.

Pick up the trail on the right (north) side of the park road at about 0.2 mile from the entrance. Follow the trail north to the intersection with the orange-blazed trail. While the orange trail goes straight (north), you should head to your left (west), staying on the white trail as it heads south. Follow the trail 0.4 mile and take a right (west) at the beach area. The trail begins to head north again and crosses over the Blackledge River on a bridge. Follow to a stone wall and then turn left (west). The trail then goes along French Road and heads south for

11/ Gay City State Park

The entrance to Gay City State Park is on the west side of Route 85 in the township of Hebron. It is most easily reached from the junction of Route 94 with Route 85 in Hebron. From the junction follow Route 85 north 1.9 miles to the park entrance. Approaching from the north on Route 85, continue south from the Bolton–Hebron boundary line 0.7 mile to the park entrance. A variety of blazed trails, ranging from easy to not-too-difficult, course through the park, as well as in the adjoining Meshomasic State Forest. Enter the park and follow signs to parking lots near the pond.

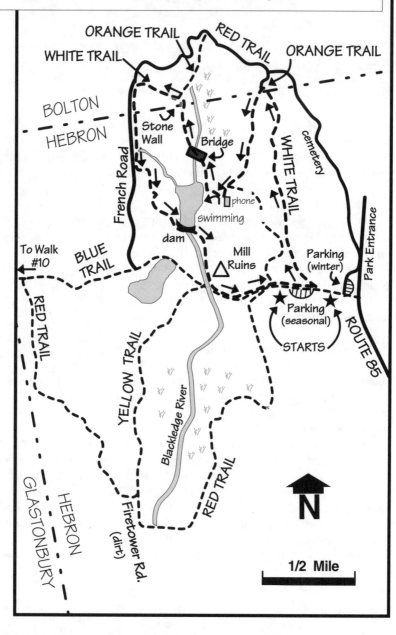

A GHOSTLY HISTORY

The area is full of history, even including two ghost tales—one of a peddler who was murdered and his body thrown in a charcoal pit to destroy the evidence, and another of a helper killed outright by his blacksmith overseer when he showed up late for work.

A small cemetery located near the entrance to the park marks the approximate spot of the resting places of some former area residents. The stones are originals, but they have been moved from time to time and may not actually mark the exact graves.

0.3 mile, where it leaves the old road and crosses a small stream. Follow the white blazes as the trail continues south past stone ruins of a paper mill on the left (east) side of the trail. Today, the foundations looks much like a lost city, draped with wild grapevines and ivy. From time to time buttons are found here in the soil, evidence from the days when ragpickers collected old clothes to make paper—rag paper—at the site.

The trail ends at the park road. Follow it 0.3 mile back to your car.

If you've still got the energy, investigate the waterways, stone foundations, and other trails of the park. Many wildflowers can be found near the water, along with tadpoles, minnows, and abundant bird life. Look for beaver-gnawed trees—most are saplings—along the banks of the river. Old homesites, now only cellar holes, are scattered throughout the woods. Notice wildly sprouting apple trees and overgrown lilacs or gnarled loops of grapevine, planted long ago to grace a yard.

A Historical Perspective

In 1796 a religious sect led by Elijah Andrus settled in the area that later became known as Gay City. In 1800, after Andrus's departure, John Gay was elected president of the community that soon bore his name. The settlement of Gay City grew and prospered and was almost self-sustaining. At its peak the thriving colony boasted twenty-five families, with the Gay clan in the majority. There were large farms and homes, a sawmill, two grist mills, and a very successful woolen mill. There were also mills that manufactured paper and satinet, a thin satin fabric.

12

Nathan Hale Trail
Coventry

Distance: Less than 2 miles round-trip

Difficulty: Easy

Traverse quiet forest and perhaps the same ground the young Nathan Hale may have explored long before he went to Yale University to become a schoolteacher and then on to serve his fledging nation as an undercover agent. This trail is near the Nathan Hale State Forest, which surrounds the Nathan Hale Homestead lands.

Enter the path, which wanders through a grove of chestnut trees. At less than 1 mile, you can glimpse the pasture and nearby barn of the Hale Homestead through a break in the stone wall. (Imagine Hale and his friends walking and playing along these very paths more than 200 years ago!) The house is not actually the one in which Hale was born; that one was located near the red building that stands today but was torn down when the new and grander home was finished the year Nathan Hale died. Many family artifacts are on display, however, including Hale's fowling piece—the hunting gun he used as a boy—and his powder horn.

Two small ponds west of the trail are home to frogs and other water creatures as well as sphagnum moss and sedges—plants that like damp roots and boggy conditions.

The path is not blazed in any way but is easy to follow; stay on the main trail, which leads downhill, past a now-open meadow that has been logged, and on to Bear Swamp. Walk the entire path or any portion of it—the varied terrain and history make this an appealing area.

The grove of maples in front of the Nathan Hale Homestead is called the Holy Grove and consists of sugar maples planted in 1812. The name is in reference to services held under the trees by a member of the Hale family.

For an interesting, short side trip, walk or drive South Street to a spot directly across from the Strong-Porter House, built in 1730. Two

12/ Nathan Hale Trail

Follow state routes to Coventry center; take Route 6 southeast from Bolton or Route 44. Follow Cross Street to end, and turn right on South Street 1.4 miles to stop sign and fork in the road. Go left 0.4 mile to the Hale Homestead. Signs directing travelers to the Hale Homestead are numerous. Trails and historic sites lead off South Street. Park near the trail entrance, 0.1 mile west of the homestead's north entrance. Limited parking is available at the homestead lot when it is open.

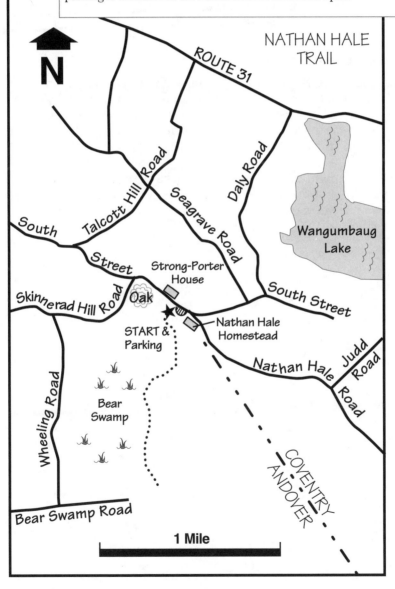

N

NATHAN HALE
TRAIL

ROUTE 31

Talcott Hill Road

Daly Road

Seagrave Road

South

Street

Wangumbaug
Lake

Strong-Porter
House

Skinnerad Hill Road

Oak

South Street

START &
Parking

Nathan Hale
Homestead

Nathan Hale

Road

Judd Road

Wheeling Road

Bear
Swamp

COVENTRY
ANDOVER

Bear Swamp Road

1 Mile

stone monuments (one to the chief forester of Connecticut, Harry McKusick, and the other to the site of the house of Asher Wright, Nathan Hale's boyhood friend and army attendant) flank an old cart path where you may park. Be sure to read the inscription about Asher Wright; it may conjure up a picture of the area as it was long ago. Just a short jaunt down the inviting path is an enormous oak—a survivor from Hale's days?

Return to your vehicle, or choose another area trail (one leads off the Hale Homestead parking lot), or visit one of the historic sites in the area.

A Historical Perspective

Connecticut native Nathan Hale was only twenty-one years old when he declared, "I only regret that I have but one life to lose for my country," and was subsequently hanged for the high crime of treason by the British. There are several sites in the state where Hale was a schoolteacher, but this walk takes you near his boyhood home and birthplace.

Captain Nathan Hale is the state's official hero. He was hanged in New York City and the location of his grave remains unknown; most likely it is under the streets of Manhattan.

13

Wolf Rock
Mansfield

Distance: 1.5-mile loop

Difficulty: Moderate

This is a good, not-too-strenuous walk with gentle inclines. It follows a portion of the blue-blazed Nipmuck Trail and passes Wolf Rock, a huge round glacial boulder perched on the edge of a 40-foot cliff in Mansfield. A connecting yellow-blazed trail makes it possible to do a loop of about 1.5 miles that includes this high rocky spot with its views of woods and fields.

Follow the blue blazes from the south side of Crane Hill Road. At about 0.25 mile, you'll come to a sizable rock. A yellow-blazed trail is at the right; you'll come back via this trail.

Continue on the trail taking the left path past the rock. You'll pass through rich woods to the stone oddity, Wolf Rock, which sits atop an outlook at approximately 0.5 mile; the trail then goes downhill almost immediately. Take a side path to the bottom of the rock outcropping. Note that this ledge is popular with rock climbers; should you see brightly hued ropes while on top of the cliff, use caution when approaching the edge so as not to send rubble down on top of the climbers.

After exploring the area, pass a battleship of a rock that looms to the left of the trail. Here, choose to take either the Nipmuck (blue blazes) back or continue farther on the yellow trail, which goes straight forward for about 0.1 mile before turning right to go downhill. Continue on this road for a short distance before reaching a right turn, then look for the yellow circles that mark the trail, and head back up the hill to the end of the loop. Follow the blue blazes a short distance to the road and your vehicle.

The Rock and the Tract

> **TRAIL TIPS** 🍃
>
> No facilities; a parking area for several vehicles is off-road on a dirt shoulder.

Wolf Rock has long attracted walkers from the nearby University of Connecticut. For even longer, it has figured in local history. Early settlers apparently named the rock after the animal that made its home

13/ Wolf Rock

To reach Wolf Rock, take Route 195 to Brown's Road (next to a white church) in Mansfield Center. Follow Brown's Road 1 mile to a fork; take the left onto Crane Hill Road. In about 0.15 mile, you'll see the blue blazes of the Nipmuck Trail crossing. Leave your car in the parking area on the right side of the road; cross to the left (south) side and follow the blue blazes.

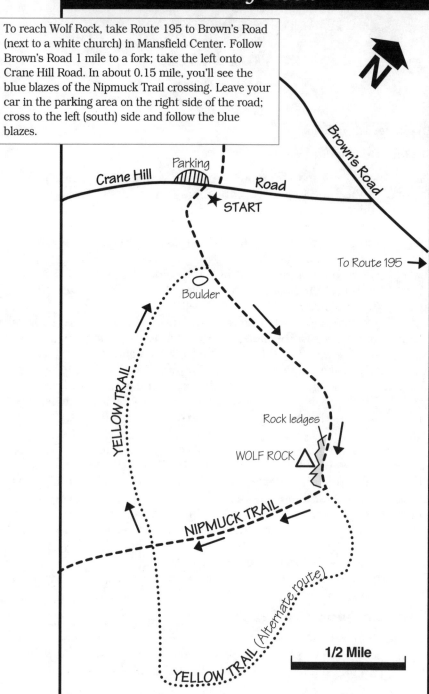

N

Brown's Road

Crane Hill

Parking

Road

★ START

To Route 195 →

Boulder

YELLOW TRAIL

Rock ledges

WOLF ROCK △

NIPMUCK TRAIL

YELLOW TRAIL (Alternate route)

1/2 Mile

there (and caused them so much worry). A stroll to the bottom of the stone cliff will allow an examination of the numerous crevices that may have served (and perhaps still do!) as animal (though not wolf) dens.

Today the rock and its surroundings are owned by the Joshua's Tract Conservation and Historic Trust. The trust, established in 1966 to preserve natural resources and areas of historical significance, is named for Joshua, son of the Mohegan Sachem Uncas. In the seventeenth century Joshua bequeathed a tract of land in eastern Connecticut to a group of settlers from Norwich. The trust now looks after more than 1,000 acres of land, many with marked trails, in the Connecticut towns of Mansfield, Ashford, Columbia, Coventry, Lebanon, Franklin, Windham, Scotland, Chaplin, and Hampton. The area covered by these towns is roughly that of the original "Joshua's Tract." In 1969 Wolf Rock and some of the surrounding land became the first acquisition of Joshua's Trust. At one time an iron observation tower stood on the rocky outlook— look carefully and you will find the iron ring bolts left from the tower.

IN THE AREA

Nearby Storrs has a wealth of eateries, including the UConn Dairy Bar for outstanding and generous portions of ice cream (best to visit on a weekend or in summer when school is not in session). See also "In the Area," Walk 14, Nipmuck Trail.

14

Nipmuck Trail
Mansfield

Distance: 2 miles one way with option for more

Difficulty: Easy

This serene walk under towering trees offers ample opportunities for river explorations. Since most of the terrain is level, the walk is suitable for families and all abilities. This excursion is especially delightful for naturalists as birds, delicate wildflowers, and insects abound along the water's edge. The round-trip for the entire walk is 4 miles.

As you get started, follow the trail in a northwesterly direction, passing some old stone foundations (including a sluiceway once used to harness water power), then through a dense stand of old pines close to the west bank of the Fenton River.

At no time does this portion of the Nipmuck Trail reach any appreciable elevation for a distant view; it compensates by remaining close to the river's edge with its contrasting still, passive pools and rushing rapids. The river, which is wide and shallow in summer and early fall, but not after heavy rain or snowmelt, has numerous sandbars and watery pockets to explore. Small fish dart about as water striders ride along the water's surface. At 0.5 mile is a wooden footbridge that will help if the trail is muddy. Other wooden bridges cross the trail where small feeder streams flow into the Fenton River. The cathedral-like trees and towering pines make this a cool, shaded walk with layers of leaves and pine needles underfoot, as well as tangles of tree roots. Ferns grow here in abundance; in spring look for the uncurling fronds called fiddleheads, which resemble the curved head of a fiddle. Keep your eyes peeled for one of the infamous flying squirrels reported in this area.

> **TRAIL TIPS**
>
> Snow or high water will make it very difficult to complete this walk. There are no facilities, and parking is in a small roadside pull-off. Nearby Storrs offers many food options and family-style restaurants.

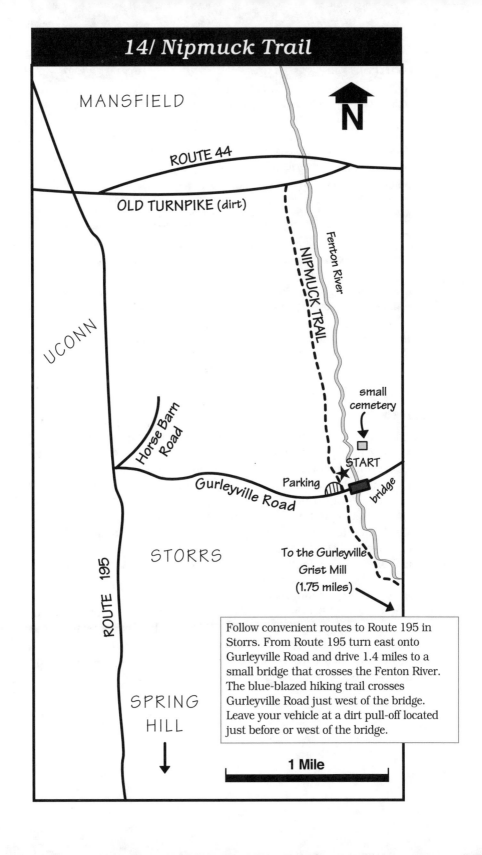

14/ Nipmuck Trail

MANSFIELD

ROUTE 44

OLD TURNPIKE (dirt)

UCONN

Fenton River

NIPMUCK TRAIL

Horse Barn Road

small cemetery

START

Parking

Gurleyville Road

bridge

STORRS

ROUTE 195

To the Gurleyville Grist Mill (1.75 miles)

SPRING HILL

Follow convenient routes to Route 195 in Storrs. From Route 195 turn east onto Gurleyville Road and drive 1.4 miles to a small bridge that crosses the Fenton River. The blue-blazed hiking trail crosses Gurleyville Road just west of the bridge. Leave your vehicle at a dirt pull-off located just before or west of the bridge.

1 Mile

Spittlebugs

It is understandable that we would be more preoccupied with the lilting song of a bird or the sight of a squirrel gliding gracefully through the air than with a glob of the spittlebug in the grass beneath our feet.

This white mass of bubbles is found on grasses so frequently that it has earned a multitude of names: bubble villa, froth castle, cuckoospit, frog-spit, frog-foam, foam mansion, et cetera. The bubbles are made by the females and young nymphs. The female makes the froth to cover her eggs. The babies, which resemble microscopic frogs, suck plant juices to use for food and to make their froth covering. The bubbles burst and must be constantly replaced.

Gently push the foam aside with a twig, and inside the mass you will see a squat, light green, froglike insect. Why this insect develops in this frothy mass is anybody's guess. It may be for protection, but the nymph is so small it would take a sharp eye to detect it. In fact, the mass of bubbles with which it surrounds itself may actually give away the presence of a spittlebug to any preying enemy.

15

Soapstone Mountain

Somers

Distance: 2 miles

Difficulty: Easy (you can drive it)

Soapstone Mountain stands in the southeast corner of the township of Somers, close to where the boundary lines of Ellington, Stafford, and Somers join. The mountain is on the Shenipsit Trail and in the Shenipsit State Forest; its elevation is 1,075 feet and its views extend over Connecticut to the mountains of New Hampshire and Vermont in clear weather.

Access to the mountain is from Soapstone Mountain Road. Park your car and follow the blue blazes as they head mostly east toward the summit. When you get close to the top, a yellow-blazed trail bypasses the summit (and a steep climb) to meet up again with the blue-blazed hiking trail on its descent. If you follow the blue trail, you'll hike a steep ascent to the top. Retrace your steps to the car.

There are many connecting trails that lead to interesting walks. A trail (just before the hairpin curve as you head up the mountain) leads off the road to an old soapstone quarry, for which the mountain is named. At the top of the mountain is a wooden fire tower, which is open to the public. Just beyond is the weather-relay station, closed off from the public by a wire fence.

> ### TRAIL TIPS
> Outhouses are located near the tower at the top of the mountain, as are picnic spots. Parking is available in a lot near the tower as well. The road leading to the mountain is open year-round during daylight hours but may be closed by snow.

Don't Feel Like Footin' It?

You can ascend Soapstone Mountain by car if you're just not up to the walk. Here's how: From the Gulf Road turn west onto Soapstone Mountain Road. It ascends to a sharp hairpin turn before reaching a fine overlook at 0.8 mile from Gulf Road.

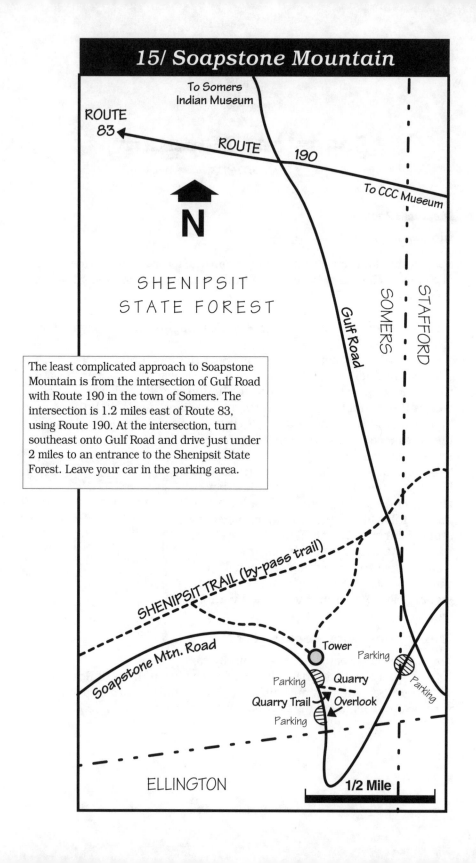

To Somers
Indian Museum

ROUTE
83

ROUTE 190

To CCC Museum

N

SHENIPSIT
STATE FOREST

Gulf Road

SOMERS

STAFFORD

The least complicated approach to Soapstone
Mountain is from the intersection of Gulf Road
with Route 190 in the town of Somers. The
intersection is 1.2 miles east of Route 83,
using Route 190. At the intersection, turn
southeast onto Gulf Road and drive just under
2 miles to an entrance to the Shenipsit State
Forest. Leave your car in the parking area.

SHENIPSIT TRAIL (by-pass trail)

Soapstone Mtn. Road

Tower

Parking

Parking

Quarry

Parking

Quarry Trail

Overlook

Parking

ELLINGTON

1/2 Mile

What Is Soapstone?

Soapstone is known as steatite or talc and has a greasy feel to it. Ex-
amples of bowls carved from soapstone (perhaps mined from this very
mountain) are on display at the Mashantucket Pequot Indian Museum
in Mashantucket (Ledyard).

16

Bigelow Hollow
Union

Distance: 1.6 miles with option for more

Difficulty: Most trails easy

Caution: The park abuts remote and extensive woodlands. Be sure to stick to the trails and watch young children that they don't wander. No matter what trail you choose, be sure to leave enough daylight to complete the walk and return to your car.

One of the more interesting trails in Bigelow Hollow is the yellow trail. Follow this yellow-blazed trail as it encircles the pond for 1.6 miles. Starting at the Bigelow Pond picnic area (0.7 mile from the park entrance) and going south, it winds along the edge of the water through picnic spots, a boat launch, and fishing areas. Footbridges provide dry footing through swampy areas where jewelweed can be found (see sidebar). For a short stretch it parallels Route 171 where the yellow blazes can be seen on the inside of the guard rails.

Walk on the inside of the rails near the water's edge, then reenter the woods on the west side of the pond. Note that icy conditions or packed snow make this part of the trail hazardous. At this point the trail requires some scrambling over rocks at the base of a wooded hillside. The trail continues along the west side on an easier but slightly hilly route, emerging at the north end of the pond. Crossing two wooden bridges over Bigelow Brook at the point where it enters the pond brings you back to the picnic area and parking lot.

There are numerous other trails and loops to explore within Bigelow Hollow State Park. Should you desire more information about other features of this popular park, speak with the ranger in charge. A detailed trail map is posted on the hikers' bulletin

TRAIL TIPS

Outhouses are located throughout the park. Picnic areas and plentiful parking are available, but on summer weekends the lots can be crowded and cars are sometimes turned away, so arrive early. Swimming is allowed in Mashapaug Pond only. There is a telephone in the park as well as a boat launch. Open year-round; a fee is charged Memorial Day through Labor Day. Bring along refreshments as this is an undeveloped area.

To reach the main entrance to Bigelow Hollow State Park, follow the road map routes to Route 171 in Union. The entrance is on the north side of Route 171 and is approximately midway between Route 197 on the east and Route 190 on the west. Enter the park and follow the service road; park your car in a designated area.

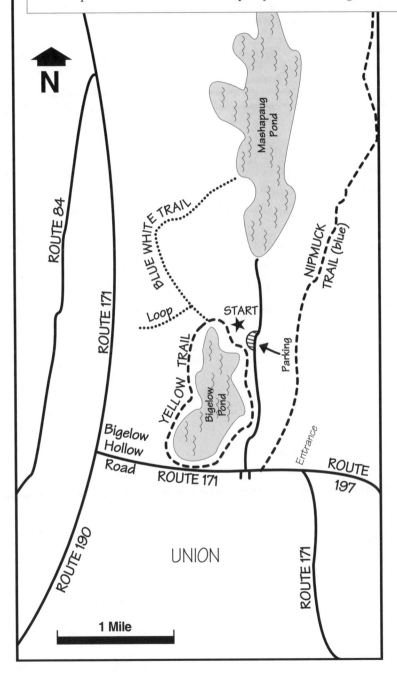

N

Mashapaug Pond

BLUE WHITE TRAIL

NIPMUCK TRAIL (blue)

ROUTE 84

ROUTE 171

Loop

START

Parking

YELLOW TRAIL

Bigelow Pond

Bigelow Hollow Road

ROUTE 171

Entrance

ROUTE 197

ROUTE 190

UNION

ROUTE 171

1 Mile

THE JEWELWEED

This plant's leaves and growth patterns resemble those of its relation, impatiens. Jewelweed's bright yellow or orange speckled flowers are worth a look, but its plump seed cases are especially entertaining. The football-shaped pods snap and explode on contact—the plant's way of spreading its seed. The plant is reputed to be an antidote to a brush with poison ivy.

board; sometimes you can find copies in the boxes attached to the boards, but not always.

You can lunch and rest at any of the numerous picnic tables or other spots in the park, or you can explore the mixed hardwood and evergreen forest. Gnawed tree stumps stand as evidence of the beavers living in the area. Note the lush green carpet of sphagnum moss that grows near the pond's edges and in cool damp spots along the trail. If you are especially observant, a carnivorous plant, the sundew, can also be found here.

The Park

Bigelow Hollow State Park is located within the 8,058 acres of the Nipmuck State Forest in the township of Union. It is thought that the park area got its name not from a local person named Bigelow but rather from the deep hollow—or "big low"—in which the 18-acre Bigelow Pond is located.

The park offers excellent recreational facilities, including picnicking, boating, fishing, and hiking.

Goodwin State Forest

Hampton

Distance: Ranges from 1 to 4 miles depending on trail

Difficulty: Easy

James L. Goodwin State Forest and Conservation Center in the township of Hampton is one of those places that needs to be visited again and again—discovering something new every time.

In the forest, there are five major trails to choose from. We couldn't decide which was the best, so here are short descriptions of each—you choose!

The Natchaug Trail, part of the Connecticut Blue-Blazed Hiking Trail System, actually starts here in the forest (it ends 19.2 miles later in Westford, but you can try a shorter walk for today). You can follow it north from the entrance and then take a right (east) onto the white trail for a loop back to your car.

The yellow trail starts at the gate and skirts the end of Pine Acres Pond as it follows old roads up to Brown Hill Pond. This is a loop trail for a total of 3.9 miles.

TRAIL TIPS

Maps and newsletters are available at the Nature Center, the center's offices, or on the bulletin board near the parking lot. Outhouses on site year-round. Nearby Hampton offers opportunities to purchase food and trail supplies.

The white trail leaves the yellow trail on the opposite side of Pine Acres Pond and hugs the eastern shore. It ties into the Natchaug Trail south of Black Spruce Pond.

The red trail splits from the yellow trail a bit beyond where the white trail starts. You can follow this trail for 1.3 miles where it then joins the white trail for a side trip to Governors Island.

On these trails, you'll have no shortage of nature and wildlife. There are butterfly and wildlife gardens to explore. Deer are numerous and beavers are active in the three ponds that have been constructed in the forest. Fishing birds, such as the blue heron or snowy egret, may also be glimpsed at water's edge.

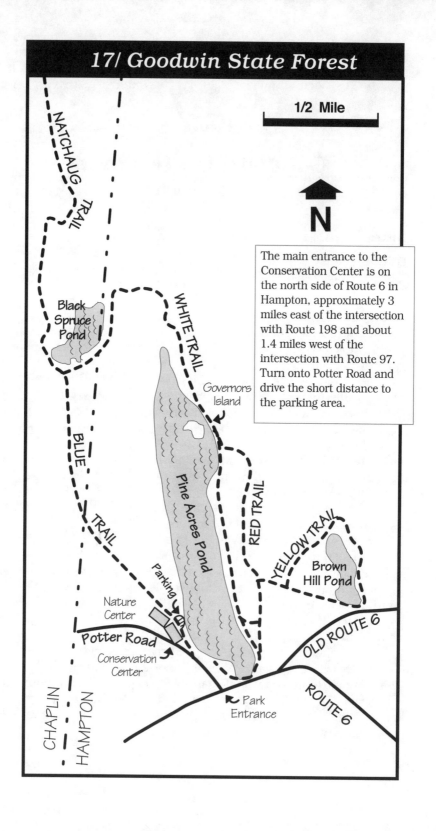

17/ Goodwin State Forest

1/2 Mile

N

The main entrance to the Conservation Center is on the north side of Route 6 in Hampton, approximately 3 miles east of the intersection with Route 198 and about 1.4 miles west of the intersection with Route 97. Turn onto Potter Road and drive the short distance to the parking area.

NATCHAUG TRAIL

Black Spruce Pond

WHITE TRAIL

Governors Island

BLUE

TRAIL

Pine Acres Pond

RED TRAIL

YELLOW TRAIL

Brown Hill Pond

Parking

Nature Center

Potter Road

Conservation Center

OLD ROUTE 6

CHAPLIN

HAMPTON

Park Entrance

ROUTE 6

It would be very difficult to get lost on these trails; they are well marked, and if you stray, you'll end up on one that will take you back where you started. So, no excuses, get going and explore; you've got a lot of ground to cover!

The Forest

The Goodwin State Forest was donated to Connecticut in 1964 by James L. Goodwin, who had formerly bought the property and developed it as a tree farm. Goodwin was a pioneer in the conservation and proper management of forests, and he started his program in 1913, three years after graduating from the Yale School of Forestry.

Goodwin's gift specified that the old farmhouse and about eighty acres of the forest were to be set aside as the James L. Goodwin Conservation Center. The center's offices are now located in the big white house, and it is operated by the Connecticut Department of Environmental Protection.

A Nature Center is open to the public on Saturday and for a variety of programs for school groups and the public.

The network of trails in the forest offers opportunities for hikers, cross-country skiers, equestrians, and bicyclists, but the trails are closed to cars, snowmobiles, and trail bikes.

Fishing and nonmotorized boating (small electric trolling motors are okay) are allowed on the ponds, but hunting and trapping are prohibited.

18

Mashamoquet Brook State Park

Pomfret

Distance: Roughly 2 miles

Difficulty: Easy

This is a wonderful walk through the Mashamoquet Brook State Park in Pomfret. Full of fascinating things to see, this walk begins off of Wolf Den Drive. Park along the road and follow it a short distance southwest to the beginning of the red trail, which is a pleasant, fairly level walk through woodlands. At a T-juncture where a map of the park is posted prominently, head left a short distance to the stone Indian Chair (taking a right turn leads to the Wolf Den). The stone chair is a two-person-size natural formation perched atop slabs of smooth rock. It's delightful to enjoy lunch while seated in the chair. After your break backtrack to the juncture (and map) and continue straight ahead on the trail to see the Wolf Den.

Pass through a swampy area filled with an abundance of ferns during warmer months; cross a wooden boardwalk, then up a hill past boulders. The low-lying area is a good place to spot salamanders and other small critters who love the cool, damp area. In spring skunk cabbage, trillium, and jack-in-the-pulpit may be seen sprouting through the rich dark muck, along with uncurling fronds of fiddle-head ferns.

The famous Wolf Den is a short uphill climb on a well-worn path with natural stone steps. Large, erratic, glacial boulders are scattered in the woods, seemingly thrown by an unseen giant's hand.

TRAIL TIPS

Outhouses located in the state park, along with picnic areas and other trails. Wolf Den Drive is not paved; be alert for ruts and use caution if your car doesn't have good ground clearance. Wolf Den has an optional access from a nearby parking lot for those who wish to shorten the walk. Pick up a detailed trail map available at the ranger station, located just inside the park entrance. Pack in your trail refreshments or pick some up in Putnam.

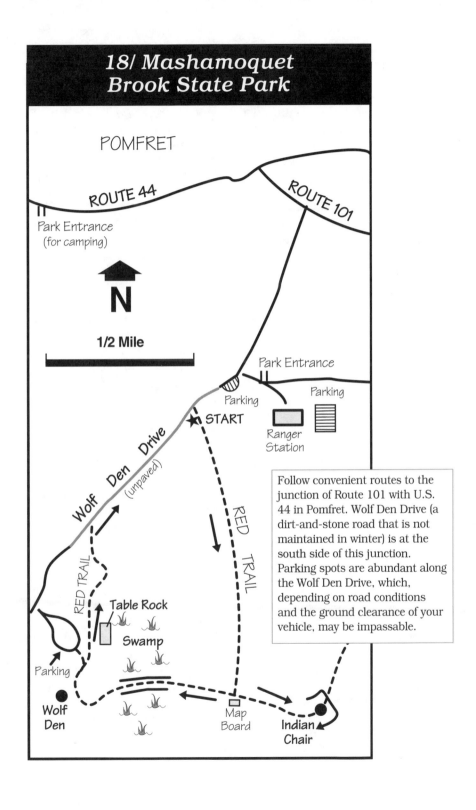

18/ Mashamoquet Brook State Park

POMFRET

ROUTE 44

ROUTE 101

Park Entrance
(for camping)

N

1/2 Mile

Park Entrance

Parking

Parking

★ START

Ranger
Station

Wolf Den Drive (unpaved)

RED TRAIL

RED TRAIL

Follow convenient routes to the
junction of Route 101 with U.S.
44 in Pomfret. Wolf Den Drive (a
dirt-and-stone road that is not
maintained in winter) is at the
south side of this junction.
Parking spots are abundant along
the Wolf Den Drive, which,
depending on road conditions
and the ground clearance of your
vehicle, may be impassable.

Table Rock

Swamp

Parking

Wolf
Den

Map
Board

Indian
Chair

The den itself is a slotlike cave. Bring the past to life by telling the story of Putnam and his exploits here (see below), and imagine what it was like to finally track the she-wolf to her lair and enter the dark narrow den—rope or no rope around your ankle.

After a break continue on the trail to Table Rock, a naturally formed "table" large enough to picnic atop and a perfect stop for a trail snack. Head north again on the red trail to the road. At about 1.43 miles from the start of the walk is a stone well now clogged with debris and sticks—but of interest because of the tiny flat shelf located inside the lip and the rock platform that was used to retrieve a bucket or bring up food kept cool in the well.

As the trail meanders along, you soon reach Wolf Den Drive; from here it's a short walk back to your vehicle.

Should you have more time, there is an extensive network of trails in the park, including a short, easy loop nature trail.

Old Put

Affectionately called "Old Put," Israel Putnam was beloved by his men and was the subject of myriad humorous, as well as serious, anecdotes. Born in 1718 in Massachusetts, Putnam as a young man moved to Pomfret, where he became a prosperous innkeeper and successful farmer. It is alleged that he answered the call to join the Continentals at Lexington so hurriedly that he left his plow halfway down a furrow in the middle of a field. He served conspicuously at the Battle of Bunker Hill. Promoted to major general, he commanded the American forces at the Battle of Long Island. He was the senior major general of the Continental Army and in command of the right wing at the time of its winter encampment from 1778 to 1779 at Redding, Connecticut. In 1779, when Old Put was sixty, he made a dramatic mounted escape from pursuing British dragoons, riding headlong down the perilous, one hundred steps carved in the precipice at Horse Neck, Greenwich. (See Walk 49, Putnam Memorial.)

Of all of Israel Putnam's flamboyant exploits, perhaps none is more familiar and renowned than his encounter with the she-wolf. For several years Putnam and his farm neighbors were losing stock to a marauding lone wolf; this wolf had a distinctive footprint due to the loss of its toes in a trap. When several of Putnam's sheep disappeared in one night, he vowed to get the wily killer and enlisted the aid of five neighbors to hunt it in alternating pairs. Two members of the team constantly and relentlessly trailed the wolf, day after day, until finally they tracked her through the snow to her lair. They tried smoking her out of the stronghold without success. Next they sent in the hounds; but after being severely mauled, the dogs would not reenter the cave.

In desperation Putnam decided to squeeze through the long, low, narrow passageway himself to confront the beast with a birch-bark torch and trusty smooth-bore gun. Tying a rope to his ankle, he crawled into the deep, dark dungeon, instructing his companions on the outside to drag him out fast if he yanked the rope twice. In the excitement their signals got crossed, and they hauled him out so fast his jacket and shirt were stripped off over his head; he lost part of his breeches and much of his hide. Removing the rope, he wryly stated that he'd rather face the wolf without friendly help. After being driven back once by the wolf, he returned later that same day, shot her, then dragged the heavy carcass out by the ears.

19

Lockes Meadow
Plainfield

Distance: 1.5 miles one way, or 1.9 miles for straight-through hike; option for more

Difficulty: Easy, but use care near watery, mucky edges

This relaxing walk wanders through woods, along marshy meadows, and next to a pond. Once you park your car, follow the blazed hiking trail southeast. The trail is primarily a woodland trail along this portion. Blazes in this area may be poor. You'll come to a T— bear left onto dirt road. Follow it to the fork; bear right just before the pond on your left. At approximately 1.5 miles from your starting point, you come to Lockes Meadow on your left. You can then retrace your steps to your car. (If you continue past the meadow, bear right at the next fork to reach dirt Flat Rock Road, alternate parking, 1.9 miles from the start.)

TRAIL TIPS

Bring along a change of footwear and clothing (especially for children). No facilities; parking is off the road in a dirt pull-off. Voluntown is the nearest town for re- freshments; pack in your trail treats. This is an isolated area; stay alert for off-road vehicles and use care during hunting season.

The southern section of the Quinebaug Trail is described in Walk 20. It is possible to walk south past the meadow to Devil's Den, Hell Hollow, and Phillips Pond and pic- nic area for a longer walk (3.6 miles) through woodlands and over interesting rock formations.

Flora and Fauna on the Quinebaug

During seasons of normal rainfall, the Lockes area appeals to a wide variety of birds and wildlife. The trail offers opportunities for picnick- ing, exploring, and nature study. Carry a camera and/or binoculars and a magnifying glass. Wear waterproofed footwear, or carry slip-on boots, should you desire to investigate the swampy area where many lovely flowers may be found.

Jack-in-the-pulpit is one of the most striking wild plants that can be found in springtime, alongside trillium (whose flowers and leaves

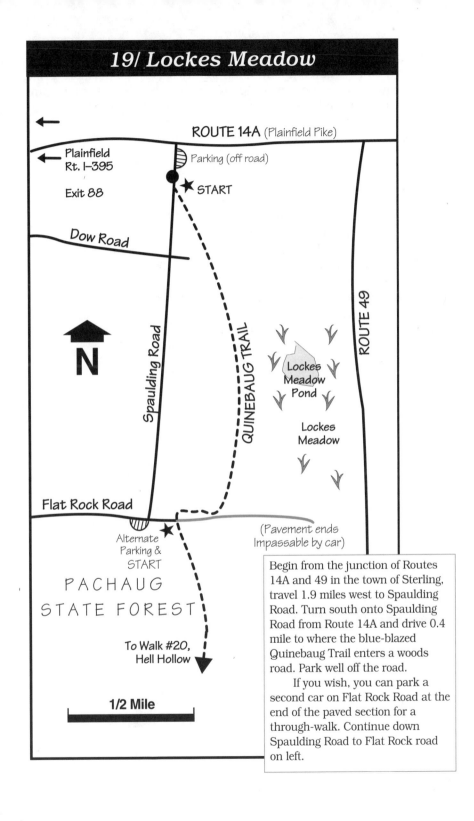

ROUTE 14A (Plainfield Pike)

← Plainfield
Rt. I-395

Exit 88

Parking (off road)

★ START

Dow Road

N

Spaulding Road

QUINEBAUG TRAIL

Lockes
Meadow
Pond

Lockes
Meadow

ROUTE 49

Flat Rock Road

(Pavement ends
Impassable by car)

Alternate
Parking &
START

P A C H A U G
S T A T E   F O R E S T

To Walk #20,
Hell Hollow

1/2 Mile

Begin from the junction of Routes 14A and 49 in the town of Sterling, travel 1.9 miles west to Spaulding Road. Turn south onto Spaulding Road from Route 14A and drive 0.4 mile to where the blue-blazed Quinebaug Trail enters a woods road. Park well off the road.

If you wish, you can park a second car on Flat Rock Road at the end of the paved section for a through-walk. Continue down Spaulding Road to Flat Rock road on left.

have three leaves or petals), violets, and other lesser-known wildflowers. To find "Jack" carefully lift the dropping "leaf" that forms the hood of this plant and see the spathe, known as "Jack," standing in his pulpit. Use care not to damage the plant. The semi-rare moccasin flower, also called lady slipper, can sometimes be seen in this area.

It is estimated that there are some 500-odd species of native and introduced wildflowers in the northeastern United States.

The hepatica, or liverleaf, prefers the leafmold soils of the high dry woodland, open woods, and forest slopes. The inconspicuous, fragile, single flowers, varying from lilac to bluish or white in color, defiantly push their way into the cold world, while their hesitant leaves remain deeply hidden in their fuzzy wrappings, awaiting more favorable weather. The frail and delicate-appearing blossoms stand the stress and hardships that often shatter their robust and hardy-looking companions.

The name hepatica comes from the Greek word meaning liver. The flower in all probability was given the name because its leaf resembles the outline of a liver. As a consequence, the plant was used as a remedy for liver complaints, perhaps because omen-conscious people believed Mother Nature was indicating the use to which her creation might be applied.

20

Hell Hollow
Plainfield

Distance: 3 miles

Difficulty: Moderate

This is a walk through woods along well-worn paths that lead around a swampy pond, over an exposed rock road, and past numerous jumbles of boulders and mysterious crevices. The short sections are suitable for all abilities, but some may tire on the longer ones—the entire circuit is roughly 3 miles.

Once you park your car on Hell Hollow Road, head north on the sandy rock path into the woods on the blue-blazed Quinebaug Trail, which follows a woods road all the way to Flat Rock Road, about 1.8 miles from your start. Flat Rock Road is well named—the smooth, road-sized exposed rock resembles a whale's back and the path follows it.

Turn right (east) onto Flat Rock Road and follow the blazed hiking trail for approximately 0.1 mile to Devil's Den. The den is a mass of jumbled boulders and ledges just off the south shoulder of Flat Rock Road. This is an interesting area to explore. Springs flow out of the jumbled rock; stay alert for the possibility of snakes and other critters in your path.

The trail between Hell Hollow Road and Flat Rock Road follows high ground; deep, sunken Hell Hollow is below to the east, and still east of the hollow is a predominant, high ridge. This woods road trail is an easy one to hike, and there are numerous ledges off the main path that invite inspection.

At about 2 miles from the start is a loop trail marked in yellow; it can be followed back to Hell Hollow Road for a total walk of about 3 miles. Be sure to periodically check for the blazes to ensure you're on the correct path.

This route requires a short jaunt on Hell Hollow Road, past the pond, to the parking lot.

20/ Hell Hollow

To Lockes Meadow
(0.6 Mile)

N

Spaulding Road

Parking

Flat Rock
Road

Devil's Den

Pachaug-Quinebaug
Crossover

QUINEBAUG TRAIL

Hell Hollow

YELLOW BLAZES
(1 Mile)

PACHAUG TRAIL

START
& Parking

Hell Hollow Road

BLUE BLAZES,
red dot (0.3 Mile)

connector
trail

Trail Road

BLUE TRAIL

PACHAUG TRAIL

Philips
Pond

Mt. Misery Brook

HELL

HOLLOW

ROUTE 49 (Ekonk Hill Road)

1 Mile

Map Directions: To reach the Hell Hollow segment of the trail, take Route 14A to Route 49 south approximately 3 miles to Hell Hollow Road. Approaching from the south, in Voluntown and Routes 138 and 165, follow Route 49 north 5 miles to Hell Hollow Road.

Turn west onto Hell Hollow Road and follow it about 1.5 miles to where the Quinebaug Trail, indicated by blue blazes, crosses the road. A large pond and swampy area, through which Mount Misery Brook flows, is on the north side of the road, 0.1 mile before the trail. Park your car off the traveled portion of highway.

From your parking spot on Hell Hollow Road, you can also head south on the Quinebaug Trail or on Trail Road (dirt) for less than a mile to Philips Pond, a lovely spot with a waterfall and picnic area.

Note: Lockes Meadow, the northern section of the Quinebaug Trail, is described in Walk 19. It is possible to continue walking north at Devil's Den on the Quinebaug Trail approximately 0.6 mile to the meadow and lengthen your walk to an all-day exploration.

21

Rhododendron Sanctuary
Voluntown

Distance: Less than 0.5 mile

Difficulty: Easy, handicapped accessible

The best time to do this walk is between June 15 and July 15, when the flowers of the Rhododendron Sanctuary in Voluntown are in bloom. Still of interest year-round, this area is alive with color during that period.

This is a nice, easy walk for all ages and abilities. The sanctuary is located in the Mount Misery Cedar Swamp of the Pachaug State Forest in Voluntown. For this walk, you'll be traveling a section of the blue-blazed Nehantic Trail that meets up with the Pachaug Trail to go to the sanctuary and over Mount Misery. The Nehantic then heads north and the Pachaug heads west.

Park your vehicle in the lot near Mount Misery Campground, and enter the sanctuary near the wooden sign H. H. CHAPMAN which denotes the area. Look for the blue blazes indicating the trailhead to the east of the parking lot.

This area is part of 2,000 acres of the Pachaug Forest dedicated on May 21, 1966, as a memorial to the late Professor Herman Haupt Chapman of the Yale School of Forestry for his interest in Connecticut's natural resources.

TRAIL TIPS

Outhouses are located in the state forest. Detailed trail maps are available at the ranger station at the end of the first road to your right upon entering the park. Pack a lunch or you can buy food in Voluntown.

A newly installed wooden boardwalk atop a built-up base allows you to sample the beauty of this area as you travel through swampy tangles of shrubs and wetlands. After investigating the walkway via a self-guiding trail, which is about 1 mile round-trip, you may wish to continue exploring the forest.

This walk can be combined with Walk 22, Mount Misery. See that write-up for directions.

To Walk #20,
Hell Hollow

VOLUNTOWN
GRISWOLD

Philips
Pond

Mount Misery Brook

Follow convenient routes to
Voluntown where Routes 49,
138, and 165 intersect. From
the intersection take
combined Routes 49, 138,
and 165 east about a mile to
where Route 49 turns north.
Turn onto Route 49 and follow
it 0.7 mile to the entrance of
Pachaug State Forest. Follow
the park road to a parking
area near Mount Misery
campsites.

ROUTE 49

Cutoff Road
(dirt)

RHODODENDRON
SANCTUARY

**Headquarters
Road**

Parking

Ranger
Station

Mount Misery
Campground

MOUNT
MISERY

Firetower Road
(dirt)

**Beachdale
Pond**

Park
Entrance

ROUTE 49

N

NEHANTIC TRAIL . . . . .
PACHAUG TRAIL — — —
QUINEBAUG TRAIL — · — · —

1 Mile

The Taming of the Shrub

The rhododendron shrub grows profusely and naturally here. Its woody, fibrous branches reach almost 20 feet in height and are thickly interlaced.

Whether it's in bloom or not, seeing this evergreen shrub growing wild in Connecticut is a rare phenomenon. Seeing it in peak bloom season is doubly thrilling. Scan the roots and swamp area for a glimpse of salamanders or tiny frogs, especially in springtime. Mosses and ferns mingle with the curved branches of shrubs to create a primeval feel.

22

Mount Misery
Voluntown

Distance: Approximately 3 miles round-trip

Difficulty: Moderate, some climbs, difficult terrain

(See map for Walk 21)

Don't let the name deter your walk. Mount Misery is a delightful, rewarding, and not too strenuous walk. The blue-blazed trail that passes over Mount Misery is the combined Pachaug and Nehantic Trails, joined for about 1.75 miles to follow the same course.

To start this walk, park your vehicle in the lot near Mount Misery Campground. Watch for the blue blazes and the trail through the woods and across small wooden footbridges. You'll pass the trail for

> **TRAIL TIPS**
>
> Outhouses are located in the state forest. Detailed trail maps are available at the ranger station at the end of the first road to your right upon entering the park. Pack a lunch or buy food in Voluntown.

the Rhododendron Sanctuary, which is 0.25 mile from here (see Walk 21). Follow blue blazes as the trail loops right onto a service road then left onto a woods road. The trail enters the woods as it ascends Mount Misery, which is 441 feet high at its summit. Be careful as part of the trail passes over bald rock and could be slippery. From the top of Misery, you'll have seasonal views of Voluntown and Sterling as well as great views of the state forest. The trip to the summit and back to your car is about 3 miles.

> ### A LITTLE HINT
>
>
> You can also cover most of this hike in your car if you feel like cheating. You can enter the state park and follow Headquarters Road (paved) northwest to its end. From there travel 0.5 mile on Cutoff Road and then turn left (south) onto Firetower Road. At another 0.5 mile, you'll come to the service road to Mount Misery on your left. You can park and travel to the summit on foot by following the blue blazes of the Nehantic Trail.

The Forest

Pachaug State Forest is the largest of the Connecticut state forests and comprises about 24,000 acres, most in the towns of Griswold, North Stonington, and Voluntown. The forest has much to offer: hiking, camping, boating, swimming, botany, geology, and bridle paths.

Geologically Speaking

Pachaug State Forest has unusual geological and botanical specimens. The great rhododendrons, Atlantic white cedar, and bearberry—all rare plants for Connecticut—will delight botanists. For the geologist are kettle holes in streams and the well-defined ridges known as eskers. Eskers are serpentine ridges of sand and gravel believed to have been formed 20,000 years ago by streams under or in the glacial ice that once covered New England. It is believed that the action of the glaciers is responsible for the botanical and geological oddities found in the area today.

23

Green Falls Pond
Voluntown

Distance: 4 miles round-trip

Difficulty: Challenging due to difficult terrain

This walk involves navigation of slippery rocks and some difficult terrain. It is not advisable for children or for those without stamina and experience. A round-trip journey is about 4 miles and will easily take most of a day.

Once you park your car, follow the self-guiding Narragansett Trail north. Descend from the road and reach Green Falls River in a cool glen. Follow the river north and cross on the stepping stones (which pose a problem when the waters are cold and the river is high). Continue to follow the river through a gorgeous ravine that narrows and winds through boulder-peaked crags and hemlock-shrouded passes. The trail clings to the river for 0.5 mile then reaches the stone dam at Green Falls Pond. The trail continues to the east, involving a scramble up a hill. There is a walkway atop the dam and an overlook of the area. Continue to follow the blazes along the shoreline, and enter the woods again. Follow a stone wall to the end. Follow the trail to the left; markers are hard to see at this point.

The blue-and-orange and blue-and-red trails (which lead to the beach area) branch off the main trail in this section. Stay alert and keep to the blue-blazed trail. Zigzag through woods past a lean-to shelter, then to the ruins of a small old mill about 1.5 miles from the pond area.

Traverse boulder outcrops, a bouncy footbridge near cold springs, and reach a massive whalelike, rocky hill at 2 miles. Underneath are the Dinosaur Caves—look for a small sign that points downward to a side path and the caves; this area can get boggy and wet.

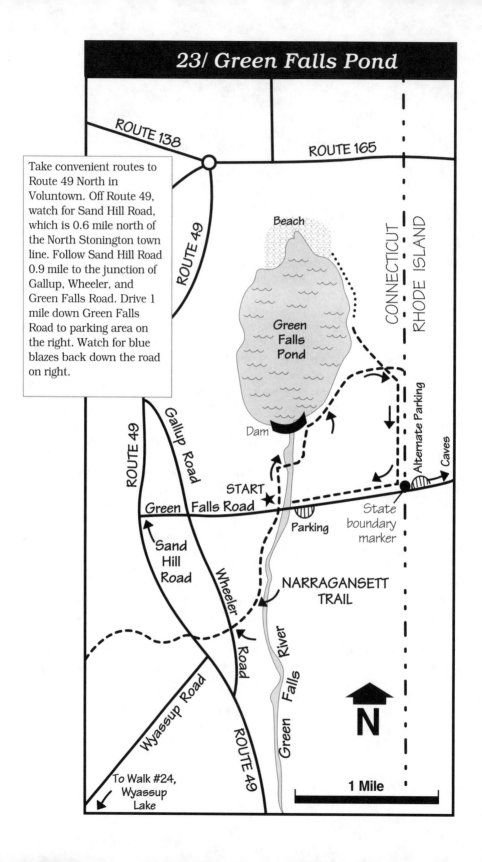

ROUTE 138

ROUTE 165

ROUTE 49

Take convenient routes to Route 49 North in Voluntown. Off Route 49, watch for Sand Hill Road, which is 0.6 mile north of the North Stonington town line. Follow Sand Hill Road 0.9 mile to the junction of Gallup, Wheeler, and Green Falls Road. Drive 1 mile down Green Falls Road to parking area on the right. Watch for blue blazes back down the road on right.

Beach

Green Falls Pond

CONNECTICUT

RHODE ISLAND

Gallup Road

ROUTE 49

Dam

Alternate Parking

Caves

START

Green Falls Road

Parking

State boundary marker

Sand Hill Road

Wheeler Road

NARRAGANSETT TRAIL

Green Falls River

Wyassup Road

ROUTE 49

N

To Walk #24, Wyassup Lake

1 Mile

IN THE AREA

Wyassup Lake (Walk 24) is nearby; continue on Route 49 south to Wyassup Road, turn east (right) and follow to Wyassup Lake Road (dead end). See Walk 24 for directions.

The trail continues to Green Falls Road. Once on the road you'll come to a granite marker that denotes the Rhode Island–Connecticut state line—now's your chance to stand with a foot in each state.

Follow Green Falls Road west about 1 mile to your parked vehicle. *Caution:* At least one road branches off to the left (south); keep to the main road. The completed loop is about 4 miles long.

Wyassup Lake
North Stonington

Distance: 1.2 to 2.6 miles one way

Difficulty: Easy to difficult depending on how far you go

This walk features huge vistas and tiny wildflowers. After parking, look for blue blazes along the road (the Narragansett Trail follows the road for a short distance). The trail then turns off onto a woods road with a metal bar blocking access to vehicles. The wide and sandy trail follows this road for 0.2 mile. The trail zigzags under downed trees, through a swamp, and up a steep climb. It then passes over a stone wall to High Ledge Lookout, which offers seasonal views across Wyassup Lake to Westerly, Rhode Island, and the ocean. Starlike asters are a common sight along the trail in late summer and autumn. The area is attractive for recreational boating and vacation homes.

You can then retrace your steps to the car at this point for a total round-trip of about 1.5 miles, or you can continue north for about 1.4 miles to a side trail that leads off to Bullet Ledge and more views. You will have to negotiate a steep climb at about 1.3 miles to get to the ledge. Just before the climb, however, look to the right (east) for "Bear Cave," a fault cave. Ascend to the summit and enjoy the views before retracing your steps for a total round-trip of 5.2 miles. The Narragansett Trail continues north for 7.6 miles to its end at Pendleton Hill.

Snakes Live in Connecticut Woods

While out hiking, it's a good practice to look where you are stepping. Snakes make their homes in the woods and fields of Connecticut, although they are naturally afraid of people and will leave an area if given a chance. Only two poisonous snakes live in the state: copperheads and timber rattlesnakes. Most bites are caused when a snake is stepped on and the animal bites in self-defense. Avoid the situation altogether by practicing common sense—especially in spring, when snakes are stretching and sunning after denning-up over winter, and in autumn, when snakes are on the move to find shelter for the approaching winter. Instruct fellow walkers to have healthy respect for the reptiles; the best prevention is education and awareness. —C.B.

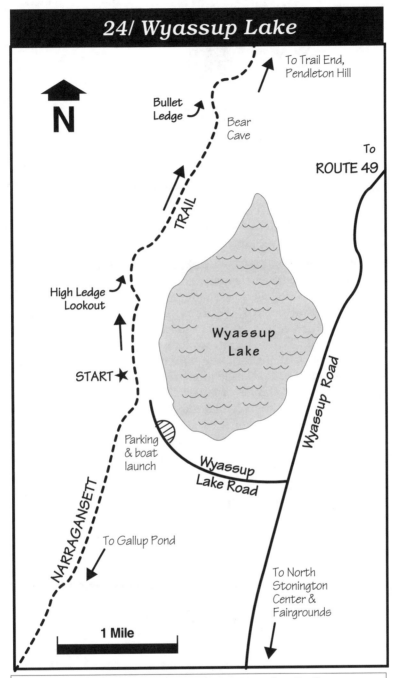

N

To Trail End,
Pendleton Hill

Bullet
Ledge

Bear
Cave

To
ROUTE 49

TRAIL

High Ledge
Lookout

Wyassup
Lake

START ★

Parking
& boat
launch

Wyassup
Lake Road

Wyassup Road

NARRAGANSETT

To Gallup Pond

To North
Stonington
Center &
Fairgrounds

1 Mile

From I–95 North take exit 92. Take left onto Route 2 in North
Stonington. Follow Route 2 for about 1 mile, then take a right onto
Wyassup Road. From the village store follow Wyassup Road north for 3
miles to Wyassup Lake Road on the left. Follow this road and watch for
signs to the boat launch and limited parking.

25

Wintechog Hill
North Stonington

Distance: 1.6 miles one way, 3.3-mile loop if combined with Lantern Hill, Walk 26

Difficulty: Easy

Wintechog Hill is a woodland walk to a quiet pond alongside stone walls. Suitable for all abilities, this walk is at the western end of the Narragansett Trail. The trail rises and dips as it traverses the entire length of the hill, east and west, a distance of almost 2 miles.

Park your car on the left BEFORE the transfer station on Wintechog Hill Road. (There is no parking in the transfer station.) The trailhead is located opposite the driveway to the transfer station. Watch for the blue blazes and follow the trail along a well-defined woods road through a lovely tangle of laurel. The trail bears right shortly, then left at the height of the land and follows an old stone wall boundary. Emerging from the woods, the trail descends and follows the south border of a field until it reaches Gallup Pond and combined Routes 2 and 201.

> **TRAIL TIPS** 🍃
> No trail facilities are available. Parking is on the shoulder of the road.

The pond may be crossed on the dam at its south end. The trip from Wintechog Hill Road to Gallup Pond is about 1.6 miles. You may walk all of it or return to your vehicle at any point.

You can also do this walk by parking a car at each end; one near the transfer station on Wintechog Hill Road and the other on Route 2, 2.2 miles south of the village of Stonington (Route 2 is only a short jaunt from Gallup Pond). The trailhead is fairly easy to find from this end. Watch for the blue blazes.

This walk can also be combined with Lantern Hill (Walk 26) for a total loop of 4 miles, but this requires two cars to avoid walking 2.3 miles along busy Route 2. For this loop, park both cars on Route 2, one at the junction with Wintechog Hill Road and one 2.2 miles south of Stonington Village (near Gallup Pond). Starting from Gallup Pond, follow the blue-blazed Narragansett west 1.7 miles to Wintechog Hill Road. Take a right onto the road and follow it for about 0.3 mile. Then take another right and follow the blue blazes north for about 0.6 miles

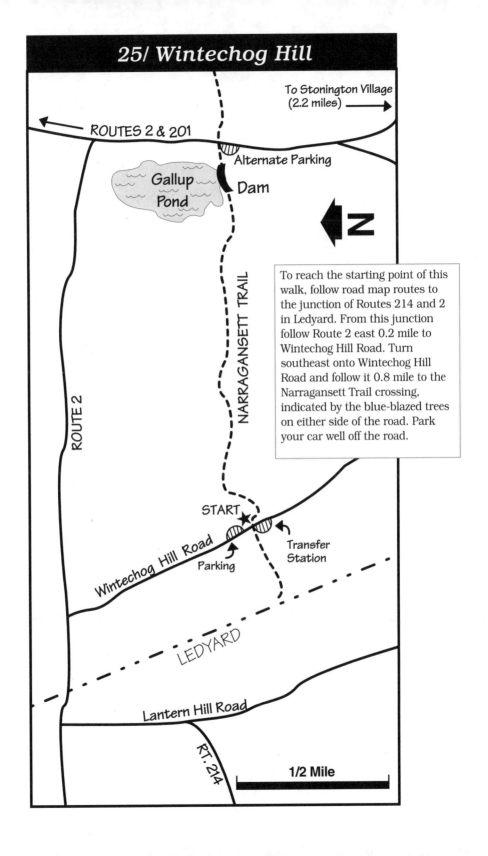

To Stonington Village
(2.2 miles) →

← ROUTES 2 & 201

Alternate Parking

Gallup Pond

Dam

N

NARRAGANSETT TRAIL

ROUTE 2

To reach the starting point of this walk, follow road map routes to the junction of Routes 214 and 2 in Ledyard. From this junction follow Route 2 east 0.2 mile to Wintechog Hill Road. Turn southeast onto Wintechog Hill Road and follow it 0.8 mile to the Narragansett Trail crossing, indicated by the blue-blazed trees on either side of the road. Park your car well off the road.

START

Wintechog Hill Road

Parking

Transfer Station

LEDYARD

Lantern Hill Road

RT. 214

1/2 Mile

IN THE AREA

For an interesting side trip to learn about the Mashantucket Pequot Tribal Nation, glaciers, and geology of the region, detour to the Mashantucket Pequot Museum. Admission is charged.

to the summit of Lantern Hill. Then continue on the Narragansett for 0.7 mile to your other car on Route 2.

Obviously, there are other combinations of this walk you can do. For example, park one car on Wintechog Hill Road near the transfer station and one at the junction of Wintechog Hill Road and Route 2, and hike from one end to the other. Use your imagination and enjoy the trails!

26

Lantern Hill
North Stonington

Distance: 0.7 to 1.3 miles one way

Difficulty: Moderate, steep climbs and bare rock

This is a nice, although steep, uphill walk through the woods across plenty of exposed rock. While suitable for most ages and abilities, it's probably not for the very young. Be sure to wear good hiking shoes; the walk involves a lot of climbing on and over bare rocks.

Park your car 0.2 mile down Wintechog Hill Road from Route 2 and follow the trail up a fair grade. The trail ascends to Lantern Hill on an old road for 0.4 mile to the point where the Pequot Trail, coming from the right (west) joins up with the blue-blazed Narragansett Trail. Continue south, ascending steeply to the summit, about 0.7 mile from the start. A trail branches off to the right (north) and leads right over the edge of the rock face; use caution as the drop-off is quite steep.

The crest of Lantern Hill is about 470 feet above sea level, presenting distant views, on clear days, of Block and Fishers Islands, Montauk Point, Norwich, and the far away hills.

Dominating the view from the summit is the Mashantucket Pequot Museum (worth a visit if you have the time) and its viewing spire, along with towering hotels and the casino. The mountain to the west is nearly sliced in half from a now-defunct silica quarry operation.

When you're done looking into the distance, check out what's beneath your feet. Atop the mountain are exposures of spiny knobs of quartz. Look for the small glittering crystals that may be observed in crevices.

You can retrace your steps from here for a round-trip distance of about 1.4 miles. Should you wish to extend your walk beyond the summit, follow the trail south and then east, descending through woods and heavy laurel growth approximately 0.6 mile

> **TRAIL TIPS** 🍃
>
> No facilities are available. Parking is off the side of the road. Food and drinks can be found in Ledyard Center, Route 117.

to Wintechog Hill Road (alternate parking). The round-trip from your car to this point is slightly more than 2.5 miles. (See Wintechog Hill Walk [Walk 25] for more options.)

26/ Lantern Hill

Follow convenient route to the junction of Route 2 and Route 214 in Ledyard. Route 214 ends by the casino. Go 0.2 mile beyond the junction to Wintechog Hill Road. Turn right (south) onto Wintechog Hill Road. Travel 0.2 mile to where the trail leaves the road and enters the woods. Park your car well off the road.

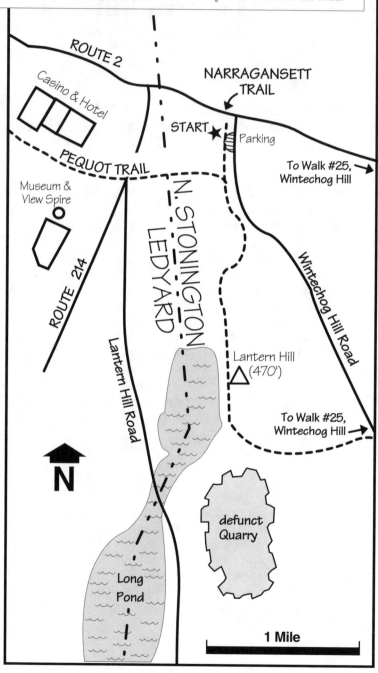

ROUTE 2

Casino & Hotel

NARRAGANSETT TRAIL

START

Parking

PEQUOT TRAIL

To Walk #25, Wintechog Hill

Museum & View Spire

ROUTE 214

N. STONINGTON
LEDYARD

Wintechog Hill Road

Lantern Hill Road

Lantern Hill
△ (470')

To Walk #25, Wintechog Hill

N

defunct Quarry

Long Pond

1 Mile

Earth Science Anyone?

The U.S. Silica Company once operated the quarry, known as the only pure-white silica mine in the east. Twenty-five grades of the white aggregate, sands, and flours were produced from a unique, enormous deposit of white quartz that was drilled, blasted, crushed and kiln-dried, then ground, screened, and air-cleaned to be used for buildings, highways, landscaping, and glass. The dictionary defines silica as silicon dioxide appearing as quartz, sand flint, and agate. The word comes from Latin *silex*, meaning flint.

A tremendous lode of silica is massed in this area. Numerous fault lines intersect here. At one time an injection of molten rock flowed through cracks and faults to eventually cool; over eons of time and through erosion, the mass of quartz became exposed and known as Lantern Hill. The blaze of white quartz outcroppings on this hill can be seen from out at sea and was once used as a landmark for mariners.

The vein of silica, of which Lantern Hill is composed, is now owned by the Mashantucket Pequot Tribal Nation.

A Historical Perspective

The hill is also reported to be a place of special meaning to Native Americans. Saccacus, a Pequot chieftain, is said to have stood on this summit to look for campfires of hostile tribes in his war against former tribesman Uncas and the Mohegans.

Early Warning from Lantern Hill

Lantern Hill is also known as Tar Barrel Hill, due to an incident during the War of 1812.

Barrels of tar were brought to the top of the hill to be used as an early warning system in the event of a British attack from the sea. The tar was to be ignited to blaze a warning if the British were spotted.

That day came on August 11, 1814, when the tar was lit to warn nearby inhabitants that British naval ships were massed in the harbor, ready for an assault. The attack never materialized since the locals were so well prepared. The English pounded the coast with cannons to no real effect—the town was well defended and the English set sail. —*C.B.*

27

Bluff Point State Park and Coastal Reserve

Groton

Distance: 4 miles

Difficulty: Easy

Voted "Best Getaway in Connecticut" by *Connecticut Magazine* in 2000, Bluff Point State Park and Coastal Reserve does not disappoint. Here you can explore an almost 4-mile loop trail through woodlands, wetlands, and shoreline as it leads you to a nearly 1-mile-long beach on Long Island Sound and the bluff for which the park was named.

The self-guiding trail starts near the park entrance and heads south past the site of the historic homesite of Governor John Winthrop, whose family farmed the peninsula in the eighteenth century. Watch carefully for the ruins off to the left of the trail.

From the homesite, continue on to Bluff Point. If you choose, you can descend from Bluff Point to two beaches, Bluff Point and Bushy Point. If it's low tide, you may find myriad tracks of various shorebirds as well as those of deer.

When you're done exploring, head back to the trail and follow it as it weaves back along the Poquonock River and to your car.

The reserve's 806 acres are closed to motorized traffic, keeping it the perfect retreat from civilization. Instead, its inhabitants include deer, raccoon, piping plovers, and other sea, shore, and woodland birds who live among the red cedars, wild grapes, greenbrier, sassafras, bittersweet, and honeysuckle that you'll find spread throughout.

Fishing, sunbathing, and picnicking are all popular activities at this reserve. It's open year-round, 8:00 A.M. to sunset and is free of charge to explore.

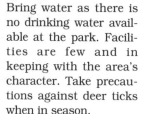

TRAIL TIPS

Bring water as there is no drinking water available at the park. Facilities are few and in keeping with the area's character. Take precautions against deer ticks when in season.

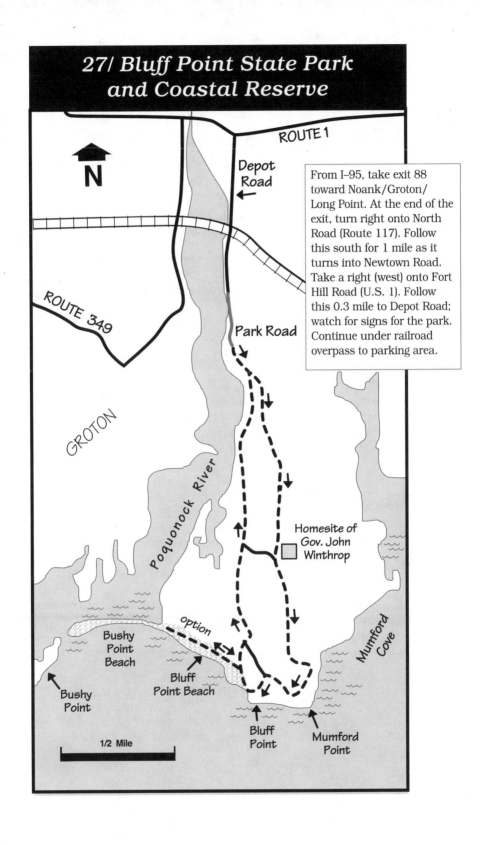

27/ Bluff Point State Park and Coastal Reserve

ROUTE 1

Depot Road

ROUTE 349

Park Road

GROTON

Poquonock River

From I–95, take exit 88 toward Noank/Groton/Long Point. At the end of the exit, turn right onto North Road (Route 117). Follow this south for 1 mile as it turns into Newtown Road. Take a right (west) onto Fort Hill Road (U.S. 1). Follow this 0.3 mile to Depot Road; watch for signs for the park. Continue under railroad overpass to parking area.

Homesite of Gov. John Winthrop

Mumford Cove

option

Bushy Point Beach

Bluff Point Beach

Bushy Point

Bluff Point

Mumford Point

1/2 Mile

28

Day Pond–Salmon River
Colchester

Distance: Up to 4.9 miles possible with small loop options available

Difficulty: Easy

In colonial times the Day family created a pond to provide water for a sawmill, where they turned chestnut, maple, and oak logs into lumber. By the 1870s horses were hauling wagons across a covered bridge over the nearby Salmon River. Today the beautiful area in Colchester is known as Day Pond State Park, and it offers lots of opportunity for exploring.

Fishermen, swimmers, and walkers head for the old Day Pond Road and the blue-blazed Salmon River Trail, which offers 4.9 miles of hiking on an assortment of routes, including one that leads down to the weathered Comstock Bridge, built in the 1870s.

Inside the park, near where the pavement ends, is a gate and a granite marker that reads ARNOLD RAVINE WILDERNESS AREA. About 100 yards beyond, the Salmon River Trail crosses Day Pond Road, an old dirt road. You can hike the old road itself, the trail's north loop, its south loop (with its Comstock Bridge connector), or any combination thereof. Each loop section is about 2 miles long; the connector is about 1.5 miles.

The north loop goes up and down through the woods. The old road (which becomes very rutted and is sometimes very wet) leads to a view of the Salmon River from the site of an old bridge. After a mile or so, the south loop passes a pipeline easement—an open, rocky stretch. Just beyond the easement, a little wooden sign points left to the Comstock Bridge. (Beyond the sign the regular trail continues back to the park road.)

The connector trail heads through woods and then follows a bank high above the Salmon River with wonderful views of the sloping bank

> **TRAIL TIPS**
>
> Picnic spots and outhouses are located in the park. There are no facilities near Old Comstock Bridge (an optional start), but across the road is Salmon River State Forest, which offers picnic areas and outhouses. Nearby East Hampton has places to pick up trail food.

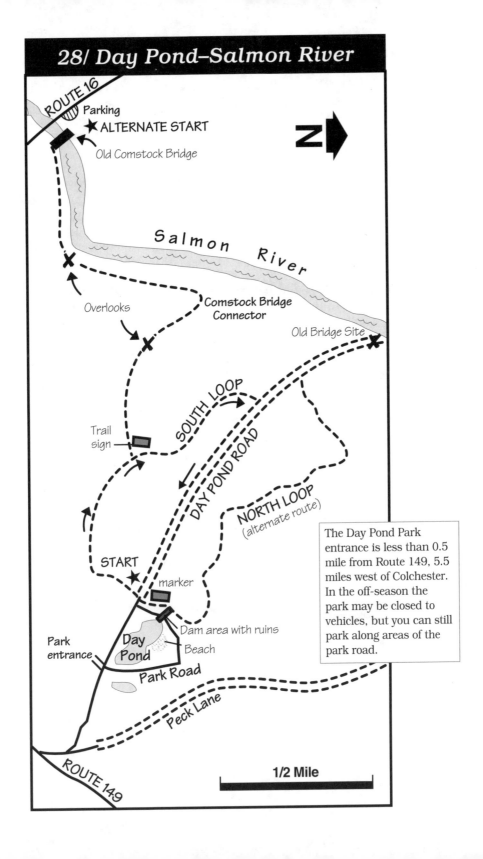

ROUTE 16

Parking

★ ALTERNATE START

Old Comstock Bridge

N

Salmon River

Overlooks

Comstock Bridge
Connector

Old Bridge Site

SOUTH LOOP

DAY POND ROAD

Trail
sign

NORTH LOOP
(alternate route)

START

marker

Dam area with ruins

Park
entrance

Day
Pond

Beach

Park Road

Peck Lane

ROUTE 149

1/2 Mile

The Day Pond Park
entrance is less than 0.5
mile from Route 149, 5.5
miles west of Colchester.
In the off-season the
park may be closed to
vehicles, but you can still
park along areas of the
park road.

(often bright with wildflowers), the bubbling river, and the hills beyond.

The trail then descends to the bridge, which hasn't carried traffic for more than sixty years but is still maintained by the Connecticut Department of Transportation. Nobody knows who the original builder was, but he used a truss-work system developed by Ithiel Town, noted bridge builder from Thompson, Connecticut.

It's also possible to drive to the bridge, which is just off Route 16, between Colchester and East Hampton (and is marked by a sign). A parking area is located next to the bridge. Hikers often start here to follow the blue blazes "backward," toward the park. The trail is on the far side of the bridge, on the left. A ramble along the river's edge can be rewarding; this area is popular with fly-fishing enthusiasts.

Bittersweet

Autumn in Connecticut is a natural wonder. Along with screamingly bright colors against the backdrop of old rock walls and green lichens, look for the twining tendrils of bittersweet. Their knobbly pods, which are a popular food for birds but poisonous to humans, open to show off scarlet centers surrounded by bright orange leaflets.

The plant uses young trees and undergrowth, such as shrubs, to clamber up into the sunlight. As the tree or shrub grows, the vine cuts into the bark, causing bulges and ridges. The resulting swirled wood is sometimes harvested and used for walking sticks.

A Historical Perspective

Once some sixty covered bridges crossed Connecticut rivers and streams; today, the Comstock is one of only three that remain. In recent times the bridge suffered the indignity of an attack by vandals, who senselessly kicked in the old timbers that had weathered over the years. Through community support the bridge has been resheathed with new lumber and its underpinnings repaired. A remote camera now monitors the stately structure, which is well worth a stroll to look out over the Salmon River flowing beneath. The route of the old road, over which many horses and wagons have passed in times past, may still be seen.

29

Selden Creek Preserve

Lyme

Distance: Almost 2 miles of trails

Difficulty: Easy

The Selden Creek Preserve in Lyme is one of the most biologically significant sites on the lower Connecticut River. Its trails are well blazed in white, blue, and yellow, and they are neither long nor difficult. A map board is located near the start of the walk in a meadow area.

The white trail leaves the parking area and extends about 0.8 mile to an overlook with vistas of Selden Creek. The blue trail leaves the white trail and heads north then west to eventually south to another overlook. The yellow trail is a shorter trail that heads out toward the pond and then loops back with the white trail.

The wooded preserve, overlooking freshwater marshes, provides vital habitat for many plants, animals, and birds, including songbirds, shorebirds, and rails. It's also a critical site for wintering bald eagles. The trails wend past birches, oaks, maples, and laurel and rhododendron plants, over lichen-covered ledges, and—in the case of the yellow trail—past a little pond (which is sometimes dry by summer's end). Overlooks on the blue and white trails offer fine vistas of Selden Creek, which separates the preserve from Selden Island State Park.

> **TRAIL TIPS**
>
> No facilities are available. Parking is located near the stone wall, off the road. Since Lyme is the town for which a tick-borne disease is named, use precautions to avoid ticks that would like to ride home with you. No dogs (except seeing-eye dogs) are allowed.

The Preserve

Until 1854 Selden Island was connected to the mainland; in the 1890s—when it was known as Lords Island—it was the site of an important granite-quarrying operation. Today it can be reached only by boat, and the preserve is the sole spot open to the public where "landlubbers" can view the creek and its marshes. The overlook on the white trail, a high rocky spot, provides an especially dramatic view.

29/ Selden Creek Preserve

- – – White Trail 4360'
- ···· Blue Trail 4530'
- ||||||| Yellow Trail 850'

All distances 1-way

To Hadlyme Ferry

ROUTE 148

To Gillette Castle

N

1/2 Mile

Joshuatown Road

Map Board

Parking

Pond

X Overlook

X Overlook

Selden Creek

To reach the preserve from the south, take exit 70 off I–95 and follow Route 156 north to the Hamburg section of Lyme. About 4.7 miles north of the highway exit, take a left on Old Hamburg Road, which turns into Joshuatown Road on your left almost immediately. Follow Joshuatown Road approximately 3.5 miles to the preserve, which is on the left. There's a wooden gate, a yellow Nature Conservancy sign, and a small parking area. (It's 1.4 miles north of Mitchell Hill Road, which is on the right.from the north, take Route 148 to Joshuatown Road; follow Joshuatown approximately 1.3 miles to the preserve (from this direction, on the right). Route 148 is the road to the popular Chester-Hadlyme Ferry, which runs seasonally. Just to the north of the ferry slip is Gillette Castle State Park (Walk 30).

The preserve is a property of The Nature Conservancy, an international, private, nonprofit organization dedicated to the preservation of plants, animals, and natural communities through the protection of the land and water they need to survive. The Conservancy maintains the largest network of privately held nature sanctuaries in the world; its Connecticut chapter protects some 20,000 acres and maintains about fifty local preserves.

The Woolly Adelgid Infestation

As you're exploring Connecticut's beautiful corners (this preserve included), you may notice an abundance of dead or dying hemlock trees. Over the past ten years or so, the eastern hemlock has suffered significant decline in southern Connecticut. Much of that decline is attributed to an infestation by the hemlock woolly adelgid. Introduced from Asia, these insects have been spreading across the northeastern United States.

The small, aphidlike insect attacks hemlocks from the base of the needles and is so small that the first indication of infestation is usually the discovery of the white, cottony egg sacs. The little beast has been able to spread throughout the hemlock population because its egg sac sticks to bird feathers and mammal fur or is carried by the wind.

Because the hemlock woolly adelgid is an exotic species, it has no natural predators in our region. Insecticides can be used, but the branches of the tree need to be thoroughly soaked and this is virtually impossible in many forest environments (although it can be effective on individual trees that stand alone). Research (and time) has shown that hemlock forests can resist and/or recover from infestation by the hemlock woolly adelgid, largely depending on other environmental factors, (i.e., where the hemlocks are located, whether there are other diseases or infestations happening, and so on.).

30

Gillette Castle
East Haddam

Distance: Varies on what trail you choose

Difficulty: Easy

The grounds of Gillette Castle State Park are no less spectacular than the castle they surround. There are several woodland trails and walking paths that traverse over, on, and across a former railroad track (along which Mr. Gillette and his guests once traveled in his miniature steam train). Others explore the surrounding woodlands. There are many miles to explore and you'll probably have to visit again to see them all.

> **TRAIL TIPS**
>
> Outhouses and picnic areas are available in the park year-round. Nearby East Haddam offers food and refreshments. Plentiful parking is available at the state park. No park entrance fee is charged. Under-control and leashed pets are allowed on park grounds and in picnic areas, but not in park buildings or on terraces, decks, or walkways leading to castle.

One trail enters the woods from the corner of the main parking lot and encircles a pond. Pollywogs in various stages of development can be seen while you look down from the wooden footbridge located at 0.25 mile. In season the banjo-like croaks of frogs chime in with a deeper jug-a-rum, the signature call of a bullfrog. Trails intersect around the pond; one passes through a now defunct railroad tunnel through a hillside, 0.5 mile from the start at the parking lot. A pond covered with pink and white lilies contains shimmering schools of goldfish in warmer months. Bridges, one-of-a-kind trestles, and rustic peeled log fencing are features to discover along the wide, well-traveled paths. (Although trails are not blazed, all are easy to follow.)

Cross the main road of the park and head west to trails that lead near the Connecticut River. In winter the patio near the castle is a popular spot for viewing bald eagles that migrate downriver to open

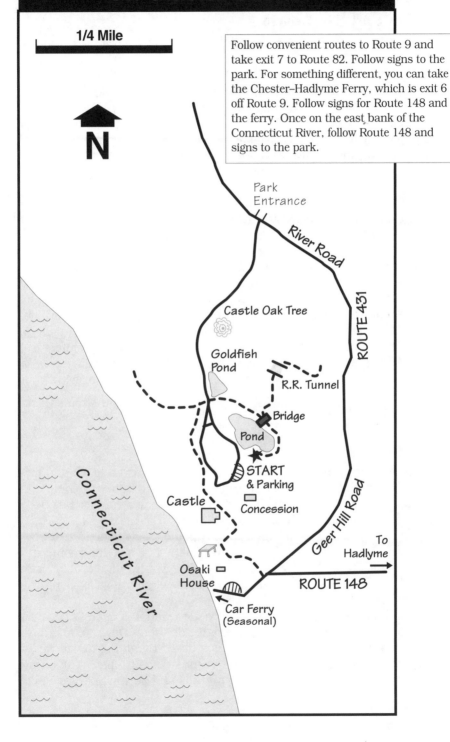

30/ Gillette Castle

1/4 Mile

N

Follow convenient routes to Route 9 and take exit 7 to Route 82. Follow signs to the park. For something different, you can take the Chester–Hadlyme Ferry, which is exit 6 off Route 9. Follow signs for Route 148 and the ferry. Once on the east bank of the Connecticut River, follow Route 148 and signs to the park.

Park Entrance

River Road

ROUTE 431

Castle Oak Tree

Goldfish Pond

R.R. Tunnel

Bridge

Pond

START & Parking

Castle

Concession

Connecticut River

Geer Hill Road

To Hadlyme

Osaki House

ROUTE 148

Car Ferry (Seasonal)

waters for feeding. The views of the Connecticut River are breathtaking. You'll not want for things to discover in this state park.

A Man and His Castle

On the east bank of the Connecticut River is a chain of hills called the Seven Sisters. The most southern of these, the Seventh Sister, rises in the townships of Lyme and East Haddam. It straddles the Middlesex–New London county line, and from its crest one looks down upon the Chester–Hadlyme ferry slip to the south.

Atop this outstanding hill, William Hooker Gillette, famed for his stage portrayal of Sherlock Holmes, built a twenty-four-room, sprawling, towering medieval-like castle of fieldstone on 120 acres. It was Gillette's semi-retirement home until his death in 1937.

The castle and grounds were purchased by the state in 1943, and together with additional purchases, they now form the 184-acre Gillette Castle State Park. It attracts thousands of visitors, who may tour the castle and inspect the interior and furnishings, which are approximately as used and left by Mr. Gillette.

Gillette personally designed the castle and most of its contents. It took twenty men from 1914 to 1919 to build the main part of the structure. It was constantly being added on to. Gillette was very particular about his castle (there are forty-seven doors and no two are exactly alike). Some visitors are impressed by the interior decorations of a past era; some are impressed—or not—by the exterior architectural style. Anyone not impressed might be described by Mr. Gillette as "a blithering saphead who has no conception of where he is or with what surrounded."

Be sure to check it out. The park offers a fascinating history of the man.

The Park

As part of Connecticut's 2010 Plan to upgrade all state park and forest facilities, Gillette Castle State Park has undergone a complete, multi-phased restoration. The entire interior of the structure has been refinished in keeping with the original plans (not an easy task, you'll see when you visit) and brought up to fire and safety code. A new visitors' center with expanded rest room facilities, a meeting room, and exhibits has been built at the park. The grounds have also been tended to, including the rebuilding of historic stone walls along the park roads.

Admission is charged to tour the castle when it is open (10:00 A.M. to 5:00 P.M. daily Memorial Day through Columbus Day; 10:00 A.M. to 4:00 P.M. weekends only from Columbus day through the fourth weekend after Thanksgiving). The park grounds remain open year-round (gates open at 8:00 A.M.), with miles of trails and stunning overlooks of the Connecticut River, selected as one of fourteen National Heritage Rivers by former President Clinton.

Ride the Ferry

As a fun side trip, you can take a ride on the seasonal Chester–Hadlyme ferry. The ferry runs between Hadlyme and Chester at Route 148. This ferry is the second oldest in the state (the first being the Rocky Hill–Glastonbury) and the first crossing here was in 1769. It takes only minutes to cross the river. While enjoying the boat ride over, you can see the seven undulating hills (Seven Sisters) with the castle perched atop the Seventh Sister.

The ferry operates April 1 through November 30. Its first run Monday thru Friday is at 7:00 A.M.; its last is 6:45 P.M. On Saturday and Sunday, you can catch it 10:30 A.M. through 5:00 P.M. There are no runs on Thanksgiving Day. A modest fee of $2.25 is charged for a car and its driver, 75 cents for each additional passenger.

31

Cobalt Mine
East Hampton

Distance: Less than 1 mile

Difficulty: Moderate, use care with small children due to mine openings

For an interesting peek into geology, native minerals, and local lore, take this walk to an abandoned mine area with old stone foundations and a small stream. It's a short walk up and down a steep-sided area. (Use caution near mine openings.)

The walk starts off Gadpouch Road in East Hampton near Mine Brook. Directly across Mine Brook, on its south bank, is a former opening to one of the Cobalt Mine shafts. The tunnel is now almost completely choked by cave-ins.

Follow Mine Brook downstream a short distance to old stone foundations—all that remain of the buildings used in the mining operation. It is reported that the mine, which was started in 1792, was never a financial success.

Near the brook and south of the state forest boundary is an abandoned mica mine. Mica, due to its high electrical resistance, is used in electrical equipment. Feldspar, used by industry in manufacturing ceramics, glazes, enamels, and binders, is also found in the area. Watch for the cobalt, which is not blue but silver-white or steel gray and is often found near mica and quartz, as well as tourmaline.

You will also find hardened lumps of what appears to be volcanic

---

Map Directions: The mine may be reached from the junction of Route 151 with Route 66 in Cobalt. Drive northeast on Route 66 for 1.2 miles to Cone Road, on the left. Turn onto Cone Road. In about 0.5 mile you'll come to Abbey Road. Jog left on Abbey, right on North Cone Road, and then go left on what appears to be Cobalt Road for 0.1 mile to Gadpouch Road on the left. (You'll have traveled a little more than 1 mile from Route 66.)

Continue on Gadpouch Road a few hundred feet to an open area on the right, between the road and Mine Brook. This, the first of two parking areas, is marked by a line of boulders. Park your car here and walk to the fenced-off, abandoned, cobalt mine excavation. (Don't lean on the fencing; it is wobbly and care should be used with young children.)

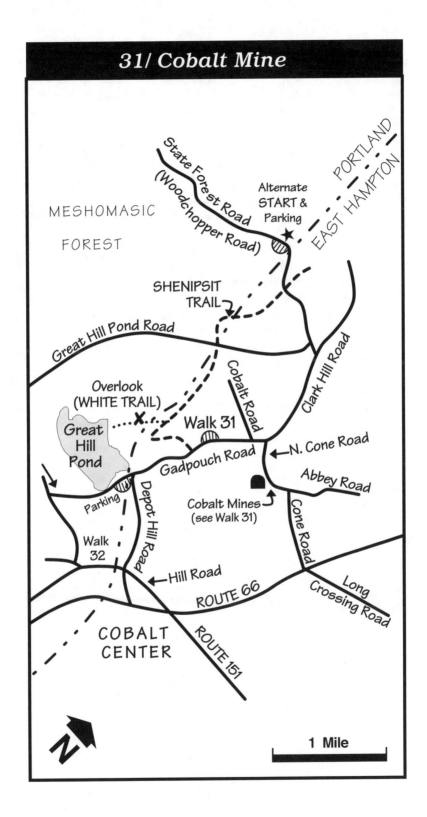

State Forest Road
(Woodchopper Road)

PORTLAND
EAST HAMPTON

Alternate
START &
Parking

MESHOMASIC
FOREST

SHENIPSIT
TRAIL

Great Hill Pond Road

Clark Hill Road

Overlook
(WHITE TRAIL)

Cobalt Road

Walk 31

Great
Hill
Pond

N. Cone Road

Gadpouch Road

Abbey Road

Parking

Cobalt Mines
(see Walk 31)

Depot Hill Road

Cone Road

Walk
32

Long
Crossing Road

Hill Road

ROUTE 66

COBALT
CENTER

ROUTE 151

N

1 Mile

TRAIL TIPS

No facilities are available. Limited parking is available off the road on dirt pull-off. Stores in Cobalt and Middletown offer trail supplies. A good mineral book with photos can add much enjoyment to a walk in this area, which is a favorite of rockhounds.

rock, although it is actually a type of slag, a waste product that results from the extraction of minerals by heating.

Watch for salamanders, which make their home in the cool glen. A variety of mushrooms also make their presence known as they sprout after rains. Shelf fungus (it looks like ears) adorns the many fallen trees that crisscross the ravine.

Cobalt: It Sounds Blue But Isn't

Cobalt was used primarily for coloring fine china, especially delftware. Cobalt is the Anglicized form of the German word kobold, meaning a goblin or gnome. The German miners considered cobalt a destructive force and a demon in their mines. They named the silver-white metallic element kobold because they thought it was worthless; and when found in combination with arsenic and sulphur, it was harmful both to their health and the valuable silver ores they were mining.

32

Meshomasic Forest
East Hampton

Distance: 2 miles one way from Great Hill Pond Road to Woodchopper Road

Difficulty: Moderate, some steep climbs

This is a terrific walk along the blue-blazed Shenipsit Trail through the Meshomasic Forest (Connecticut's first state forest).

After parking your car, follow the blue blazes northwest through the woods as the trail begins to climb. As you ascend Great Hill Ridge, the trail becomes steadily steeper. At about 0.8 mile, watch for the white-blazed trail that heads off to the left (east) several hundred feet to the bald cap of Great Hill (770 feet above sea level) and to an outlook with exceptional views of Great Hill Pond 400 feet directly below and the broad sweep of the Connecticut River, cradled by towering hills as well as the nearby town of Middletown. Once you've reached this summit, the trail levels out. This is the ideal spot to rest and lunch while taking in the scenery.

When you're ready, head

TRAIL TIPS

No facilities available. Food and meals can be purchased in nearby Cobalt on Route 66. Bring along water and binoculars—the view from the top is impressive. Wear sturdy boots with ankle protection. For more about the features of this forest, check out a video John LeShane—an area resident and avid outdoorsman—has produced about Meshomasic Forest and its history; it's available at Portland Public Library.

back to the Shenipsit and the blue blazes, and follow the trail along the ridge (the boundary between Portland and East Hampton). Continue along this trail over rocky ups and downs for about another 1.75 miles to the forest service road (Woodchopper Road). If you didn't park another car here, you can retrace your steps back to Great Hill Pond Road.

Options

If you're in the mood to keep hiking, the Shenipsit Trail heads north for another 6.2 miles to intersect with Route 2 in Glastonbury.

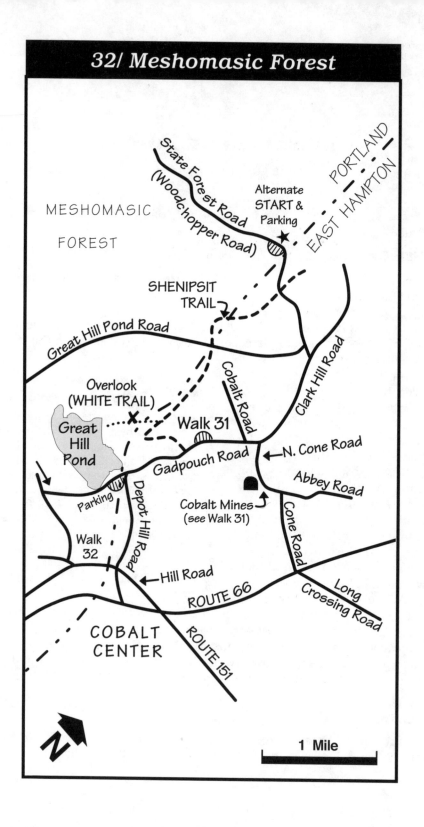

MESHOMASIC

FOREST

State Forest Road
(Woodchopper Road)

PORTLAND

EAST HAMPTON

Alternate
START &
Parking

SHENIPSIT
TRAIL

Great Hill Pond Road

Cobalt Road

Clark Hill Road

Overlook
(WHITE TRAIL)

Great
Hill
Pond

Walk 31

N. Cone Road

Gadpouch Road

Abbey Road

Parking

Cobalt Mines
(see Walk 31)

Depot Hill Road

Cone Road

Walk
32

Hill Road

ROUTE 66

Long
Crossing
Road

COBALT
CENTER

ROUTE 151

N

1 Mile

Map Directions: Follow the most convenient route to the junction of Routes 66 and 151 in the Cobalt section of East Hampton. Travel 0.1 mile west and take right onto Depot Hill Road. Travel 0.8 mile and turn left at the Y intersection onto Great Hill Pond Road (gravel). Park well off the road. Trailhead is just less than 0.5 mile on left.

For alternate parking/start: Drive northeast on Route 66 for 1.2 miles to Cone Road, on the left. Turn onto Cone Road and follow it to Abbey Road. Jog left and then right onto North Cone. About a mile from Route 66, you reach a junction with Cobalt and Gadpouch Roads on the left and Clark Hill Road on the right. Follow Clark Hill Road 0.7 mile to a sign MESHOMASIC STATE FOREST, on the left, next to a dirt service road. Turn onto this road (called Woodchopper Road) and follow it 0.6 mile to the Shenipsit Trail crossing, indicated by blue-blazed trees.

At the intersection of the white and blue trails, you can choose to take the blue trail down to the Cobalt Mine area (see Walk 31).

Alert!

Do not bushwhack along this trail. Rattlesnakes have been reported in this area; in fact, that's where the forest got its name. The Native American name Meshomasic is thought to refer to the many rattlesnakes found in the area.

33

Coginchaug Cave

Durham

Distance: 1.7 miles one way

Difficulty: Moderate to extreme. Not for young children; trail goes close to edges and dropoffs are very steep.

Park your car off Higganum Road, and follow the trail's winding course south through the woods. At 0.25 mile it bears to the left at a junction. At 0.5 mile is a stream bed that is dry in summer, with stepping stones for crossing in other seasons. The path now begins to climb more steeply between ledges and over ridges. When fording swampy areas use the convenient stepping stones. Wild turkey and deer frequent this area; walk quietly and you might catch glimpses of them. Look out for their tracks on the trail. After crossing the swampy area on your left, the trail ascends to rock outcrop. Climb over and weave your way along cliff tops (going gets a bit tricky here—BE CAREFUL!). Watch for seasonal views off to the west.

Map Directions: Follow Connecticut road map routes to Durham center. Start from the signal light at the junction of Routes 17 and 79. Higganum Road is just beyond this intersection on the right. Follow Higganum Road for 1.3 miles to a stop sign. Take a right (you're still on Higganum Road) and travel another 0.6 to the trailhead on the right. It's a bit hard to find but watch for the blue blazes on the trees. Don't be fooled by a dirt pull-off that comes before the trailhead—that's not it; keep going until you reach the grassy pull off. You could always park on the first pull-off and walk ahead to the trail access. If you come to 567 Higganum Road (watch for numbers on the mailboxes) you've missed it; turn around and watch closely for it!

If you're going to leave a car on Old Blue Hills Road, travel 1 mile south from the intersection on Route 79. You'll see the blue and white oval sign on the left side of Route 79 indicating trail access to the Mattabessett. Take this left onto Old Blue Hills Road and follow the blue blazes along the road for 0.7 mile to the trailhead on the right side of the road. Parking is curbside here; pull off best you can.

If you want to get to Higganum Road from here, follow Old Blue Hills Road 0.2 mile to its end. Turn left onto Green Lane and follow this 0.5 mile to its end. At this stop sign, turn right onto Higganum Road and follow 0.3 mile to the trail access on the right. You'll see many yellow blazes indicating state property available for hunting.

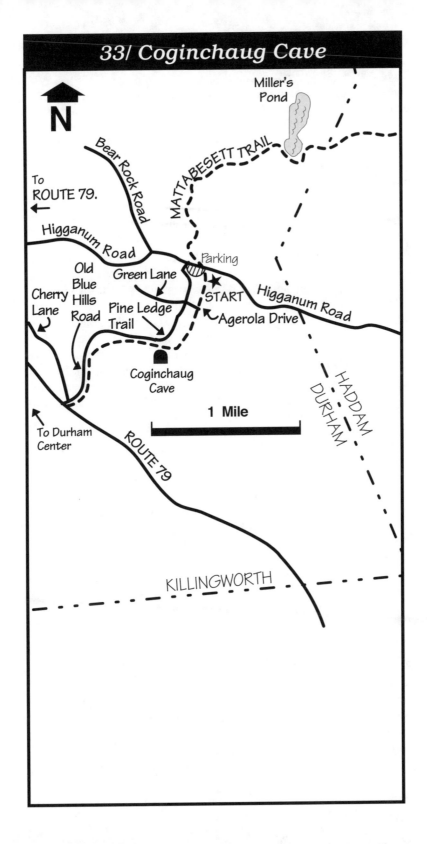

N

Miller's Pond

Bear Rock Road

MATTABESETT TRAIL

To ROUTE 79.

Higganum Road

Parking

Old Blue Hills Road

Green Lane

Cherry Lane

Pine Ledge Trail

START

Higganum Road

Agerola Drive

Coginchaug Cave

HADDAM
DURHAM

1 Mile

To Durham Center

ROUTE 79

KILLINGWORTH

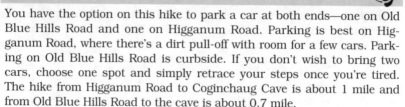
A difficult hike, this one will have you a bit winded once you get to the top. It's worth the trip, though; especially on a hot summer day as your destination is a cool and shaded "cave" with lots of history to contemplate.

The cave, actually a very large rock overhang, is approximately 0.95 mile from the trail entrance. To reach the cave you must climb a high ridge, under which Coginchaug Cave lies. Leave the ridge and descend left down a steep slope down the face of the ledge. This part of the trail is a little tricky; care should be taken, especially with young children. Within a few yards the footing eases as the path widens and leads into the cave from the south.

Coginchaug Cave is quite impressive. It is a large shelter cave, 30 feet high, 20 feet deep, and extending more than 50 feet along the base of the cliff. It has been reported that American Indian artifacts, arrowheads, and tools have been found here. You'll also see evidence of not-so-historical fires. A small brook winds through the valley; piles of boulders make for interesting exploring.

After spending as much time as you desire in the area, return to your car by the same trail or continue on the Mattabesset to Old Blue Hills Road (where you can park another car if you choose). If you continue, follow the blue blazes down from the cave, crossing several brooks to an old woods road. Follow blue blazes carefully as it's easy to be led astray.

Keep Eyes Open for Wildlife

While it is common to find deer tracks and the evidence of raccoons while on a walk, it is much more common to see small animals. Keep your eyes peeled for wildlife while out walking—evidence of a hidden world is everywhere, from chewed tree limbs to owl pellets (complete with small bones and often a tiny mouse skull) to scat (droppings) left behind on a cleared rock to mark an animal's territory. —*C.B.*

34

Pistapaug Mountain
Durham

Distance: 2.4 miles one way

Difficulty: Moderate, some tricky terrain, steep dropoffs; not for toddlers, small children

Pistapaug Mountain is located on the Mattabesett Trail in the town of Durham, west of Route 17. You may park a car at either end of this 2.4-mile hike (one on Route 17 and one on Howd Road), or you can leave one car and simply retrace your steps.

To access the trail from Route 17, begin at the intersection of Routes 79 and 17 in Durham center. Travel approximately 3.5 miles south on Route 17, and watch for small highway bridge and cement blocks on right (west) side a very short distance past Forline Drive. You'll have to pull well off the road to park safely.

Look for the blue blazes of the Mattabesett Trail, and follow them into the woods. The trail soon crosses a small brook

TRAIL TIPS

This is a walk that requires good shoes with adequate ankle support. The trails are littered with loose trap rock and can be tricky.

There are steep dropoffs; be careful especially with small children.

No facilities are available. Parking is off the side of a busy road. Nearby Durham offers food and refreshment possibilities.

over rocky outcrops, then continues north along the brook for about 100 yards. Watch for blue blazes carefully; many side trails can lead you astray. After bending left, it follows an old woods road south a short distance before turning north and then up to the ridge of Pistapaug Mountain. The top of the mountain is about 1 mile from where you have parked. Follow the marked trail north to the edge of the bluffs, elevation 700 feet, for a view of Pistapaug Pond, hundreds of feet below. To the west and south of these openings is a grand view of gently rolling farmland—irregularly shaped fields dotted with houses, barns, and silos. Enjoy the vistas of Whirlwind Hill Road's farmlands in Wallingford and the westward mountains on the horizon.

The trail continues down a steep woods road to Paug Gap, 2.4 miles from your starting point. Here the trail crosses Howd Road (alternate parking), then steeply ascends Fowler Mountain and continues

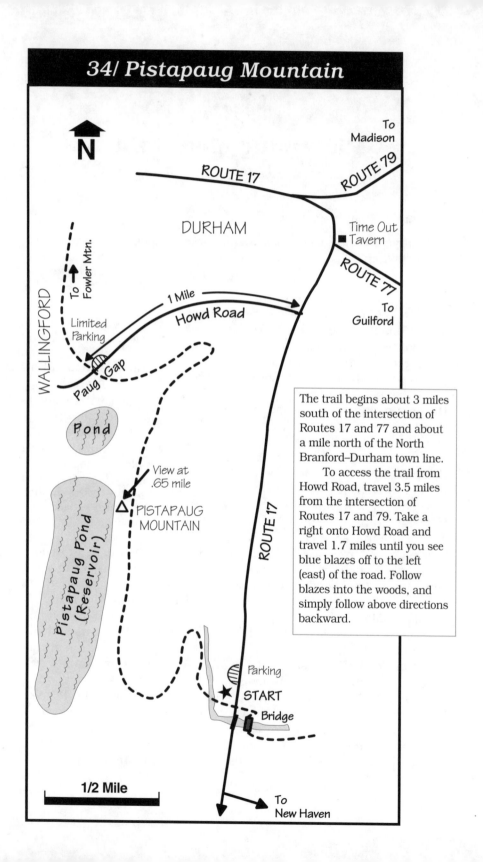

34/ Pistapaug Mountain

N

To Madison

ROUTE 79

ROUTE 17

DURHAM

Time Out Tavern

ROUTE 77

To Guilford

To Fowler Mtn.

WALLINGFORD

1 Mile

Howd Road

Limited Parking

Paug Gap

Pond

View at .65 mile

PISTAPAUG MOUNTAIN

Pistapaug Pond (Reservoir)

ROUTE 17

The trail begins about 3 miles south of the intersection of Routes 17 and 77 and about a mile north of the North Branford–Durham town line.

To access the trail from Howd Road, travel 3.5 miles from the intersection of Routes 17 and 79. Take a right onto Howd Road and travel 1.7 miles until you see blue blazes off to the left (east) of the road. Follow blazes into the woods, and simply follow above directions backward.

Parking

★ START

Bridge

1/2 Mile

To New Haven

4 miles to Route 68 in Wallingford (a total of 6.3 miles from Route 17)—but you can save that mountain for another day.

Top o' the Rock

Traprock ridges are home to some unusual plant and animal communities. The tops of these ridges are often like meadows rather than deep woodlands. Look for red cedar, chestnut oak, and delicate wildflowers that thrive near sun-warmed rocks. The distinctive traprock cliffs draw the attention of visitors to our state, yet many residents take them for granted. I know I did.

Signature Fall Tree Colors

The view of fall foliage and surrounding hills on this walk is spectacular. It's possible to tell plenty about trees just by thinking about crayons. Though nature's palette is much more extensive than the pigments that make up a carton of crayons, by scanning a mountainside, you can pick out trees that go by certain color signatures:

Sugar maples scream orange-yellow, an unforgettable sight especially when seen against a backdrop of lichen-encrusted rock or stone walls. Ashes are muted, purple-reds with an undertone of yellow. Oaks tend to be brown—rich red-browns, tawny gold-browns, and muddy shades. Nut trees are golden yellow. Sumacs are red, orange, and a hint of green. —C.B.

35

Hurd Park
East Hampton

Distance: 1 mile plus, depending on trail

Difficulty: Easy

A river park with meadows—Hurd State Park on the east bank of the Connecticut River in East Hampton was the very first state park site on the river. Today its 884 acres offer many hiking trails, including the River Trail and Split Rock Trail. These paths lead through heavily wooded areas; some ascend to high ground where excellent views of the river valley present themselves.

Access to the trails is gained from a small parking lot located on the west side of the road at the overhead traffic light and junction of Route 151 and Hurd Park Road.

Follow the park road past the Power Line Trail on the left and past a small parking area on the right; continue past Carlson Pond on the right and to a turnaround loop and parking area. Besides the ones shown here, there are additional trails to the river that are accessible from the turnaround loop.

For a not-too-strenu-ous hike with a lot to offer—Hurd Brook, the Connecticut River, meadows with river views, a steep wooded ravine, and abundant bird life—choose the River Trail.

In just under 1 mile round-trip, the wide path winds downhill from the parking area. It then leads past a steep gorge through which Hurd Brook flows. At this point, the woods open up to a wide meadow right beside the river; this is a great picnic spot. A variety of wildflowers enjoy the cool damp conditions at waterside, including jewelweed, milkweed, turtlehead, and dusty purple joe-pye weed. Sycamore trees

TRAIL TIPS

Outhouses are located throughout the park, as are picnic areas. In winter many trails are open to cross-country skiers. Trails are marked with signs denoting the difficulty of the route. Note that the main park entrance is gated during winter; access then is by walking the park road to trails or via the small lot near the intersection of Route 151 and Hurd Park Road. Middletown and Cobalt offer refreshments for the walk. There is an entrance fee from Memorial Day through Labor Day.

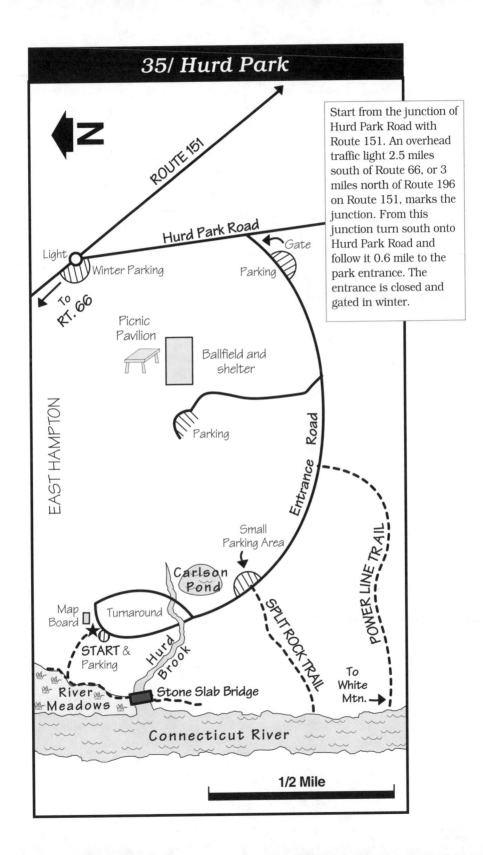

35/ Hurd Park

ROUTE 151

Hurd Park Road

Light

Winter Parking

To RT. 66

Gate

Parking

Picnic Pavilion

Ballfield and shelter

EAST HAMPTON

Parking

Entrance Road

Small Parking Area

POWER LINE TRAIL

Carlson Pond

SPLIT ROCK TRAIL

Map Board

Turnaround

Hurd Brook

START & Parking

To White Mtn.

River Meadows

Stone Slab Bridge

Connecticut River

1/2 Mile

Start from the junction of Hurd Park Road with Route 151. An overhead traffic light 2.5 miles south of Route 66, or 3 miles north of Route 196 on Route 151, marks the junction. From this junction turn south onto Hurd Park Road and follow it 0.6 mile to the park entrance. The entrance is closed and gated in winter.

with peeling, camouflaged bark tower overhead, and the ravine has a few massive trees, including once-mighty hemlocks that have been ravaged by the sapsucking woolly adelgid insect pest.

South of the meadow area is a stone slab bridge over Hurd Brook that invites you to sit down and inspect the gurgling waters, or let your legs dangle over the rushing waters. Another meadow to the south adds additional interest and viewpoints. Backtrack to the parking area and choose another trail to walk, or look for frogs, salamanders, and other water critters at Carlson Pond, near a picnic area located by the turnaround loop of the park road.

Another walk—one of the most impressive in the park—starts from the small parking area on the right side before the turnaround. Park your car, cross the park road, and take the yellow-blazed trail uphill. You'll reach a wooden sign pointing to Split Rock, a large fissure in a nearby ledge, to the right, and to White Mountain, about a 0.5 mile walk to the left. This walk offers fine views of the river and its valley.

36

Mount Higby
Middlefield

Distance: 1 mile one way

Difficulty: Strenuous to top, level once on summit

The mountain is located in the towns of Middlefield and Middletown, north of U.S. Route 66, and close to the eastern boundary of Meriden. Once you park your car well off the highway, follow the blue blazes north into the woods. The trail swings west from Route 66 to an old woods road and skirts rock rubble; the path is well worn. Another trail is marked with red and ascends through woods to the ridge. Be sure to follow the blue blazes. At about 0.4 mile the trail turns right (north), ascending a steep ridge via several switchbacks. (This is not a route recommended for small children; families are advised to use the direct route marked with red up to the peak.) To your left at 0.5 mile is a scenic view of Black Pond located at the base of Beseck Mountain.

TRAIL TIPS

No facilities. Parking is on the dirt shoulder well off the side of Route 66. Note that parking can get crowded on fall weekends. Pick up trail refreshments in nearby Meriden, Middlefield, or Middletown.

Pinnacle Rock atop Mount Higby is 1 mile from Route 66. From Pinnacle Rock one has the best viewpoint of the surrounding countryside: Hartford and Mount Tom to the north, Meriden toward the west, and a far-reaching view to the south, including Beseck Mountain, with Black Pond at its base. On a clear day Long Island Sound and New Haven are also visible. The Connecticut State Police Academy and a memorial tower can be seen at the base of the mountain, below Pinnacle Rock. Notice that the cedar and chestnut oak trees are stunted and blasted from exposure on the mountain peak. Views of Black Pond and New Dam, as well as East Peak and the lone stone tower of Castle Craig to the west (look for an array of antennae that sprout from the ridge behind the castle), are visible on a clear day.

Geologically Speaking

The bare rock formation on the trail clearly shows how this type of basalt came to be called traprock. The word "trap" is a modification of

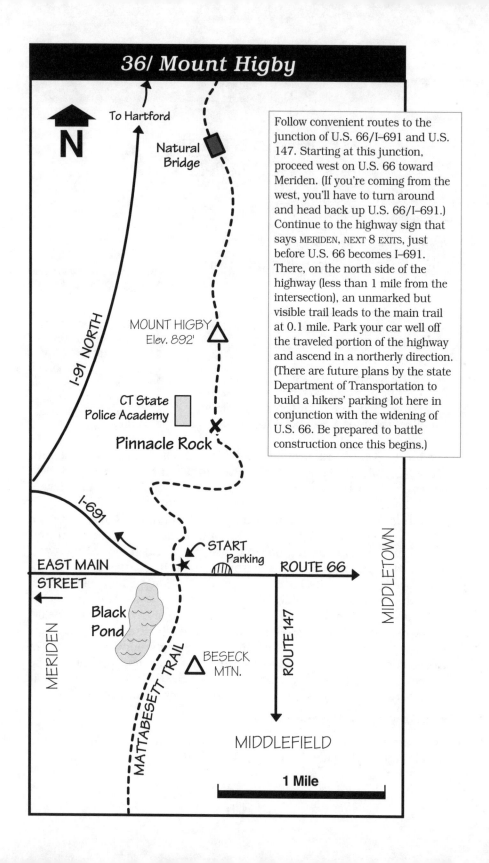

To Hartford

N

Natural
Bridge

I-91 NORTH

MOUNT HIGBY
Elev. 892'

CT State
Police Academy

Pinnacle Rock

I-691

START
Parking

EAST MAIN
STREET

MERIDEN

Black
Pond

MATTABESETT TRAIL

BESECK
MTN.

ROUTE 66

ROUTE 147

MIDDLETOWN

MIDDLEFIELD

1 Mile

Follow convenient routes to the junction of U.S. 66/I–691 and U.S. 147. Starting at this junction, proceed west on U.S. 66 toward Meriden. (If you're coming from the west, you'll have to turn around and head back up U.S. 66/I–691.) Continue to the highway sign that says MERIDEN, NEXT 8 EXITS, just before U.S. 66 becomes I–691. There, on the north side of the highway (less than 1 mile from the intersection), an unmarked but visible trail leads to the main trail at 0.1 mile. Park your car well off the traveled portion of the highway and ascend in a northerly direction. (There are future plans by the state Department of Transportation to build a hikers' parking lot here in conjunction with the widening of U.S. 66. Be prepared to battle construction once this begins.)

the Swedish word *trappa,* which means stair. As you go up and down these stones, notice how they resemble a gigantic staircase. Traprock ridges are a remnant of lava flows that shaped the landscape millions of years ago. The hanging hills you view from atop Mount Higby stand as mute testament to a succession of lava flows.

One hundred feet north of the Pinnacle is a large, bare area of basalt, quite flat, on the surface of which glacial grooves are easily distinguishable. Note how the deep scratches line up roughly north to south, the path of the glacier's flow to Long Island Sound. The grooves are the result of rocks and rubble at the bottom of the densely packed ice scouring and scraping the land as the glacier slowly ground southward.

From this point the trail passes through meadowlike areas with large boulders, then descends to Preston Notch. In colonial days, the old stagecoach road passed through this notch between Middletown and Meriden.

At 1.25 miles is a lightning-blasted cedar tree with three large limbs. The scar left behind is clearly visible.

Should you wish to extend your walk, you may continue to the northern part of Mount Higby, a stiff climb to its 892-foot elevation. Here is an interesting rock formation called the Natural Bridge. It is indicated by the abbreviation "n.b." on a small marker.

If you do decide to turn around and retrace your steps down the trail, keep the blue blazes in sight, as there are numerous well-worn, unblazed side paths that could easily lead you astray.

"No Leggers" Mean Freeze and Yield

Be careful as you walk and scramble the rocky ridges of Mount Higby. You may want to carry a walking stick and make it a habit to step over loose stone, scanning the ground as you go. Children, especially, should be warned to freeze and yield the right-of-way to any snakes ("no leggers") they might see—or think they see. Hikers should be respectful of the creatures who make their homes in the woods and ledges of Connecticut. —*C.B.*

37

Chatfield Trail
Killingworth

Distance: Less than 2 miles with option for more

Difficulty: Easy

The entire Chatfield Trail is about 4.3 miles long, but our walk goes only to Champlin Road, a gravel road that crosses the trail less than 2 miles from the start.

The trail begins on the south side of Route 80 on an old woods road. The trail enters the woods to the left after about 300 yards. The old woods road itself continues on to Champlin Road and offers a shorter, more direct route. The winding trail, however, is beautiful as it goes uphill and down, along ledges, and over a brook.

TRAIL TIPS

No trail facilities are available. Parking for Chatfield Trail is to the side of the road. Outhouses and picnic areas are located in Chatfield Hollow State Park, which offers plenty of parking on hard surface lots. The park also offers pond swimming in summer. Admission is charged from Memorial Day through Labor Day. Nearby Killingworth has places to purchase food.

The trail begins its ascent at about 0.3 mile and crosses a seasonal brook about 0.1 mile later. Follow blazes past a ledge and across a brook, and at 1.1 miles watch for glacial boulders and views to the south. Shortly after this, watch for a side trail off to the left that leads to a collection of caves. Come back to the main trail and follow it until it joins with Champlin Road. You can now retrace your steps back on the trail to Route 80, return via the old woods road or explore further by following the alternate trail, which rejoins the main trail and then the old woods road.

Mushrooms: Fungus Among Us

Most woods trails, depending upon the amount of moisture, are decorated with colorful fungi. You will be fascinated by the normal display of toadstools or mushrooms, surprised by their number, shapes, and vivid coloring. The colors range from pure white to absolute black and a gamut of shades of tan, yellow, red, green, blue, and purple.

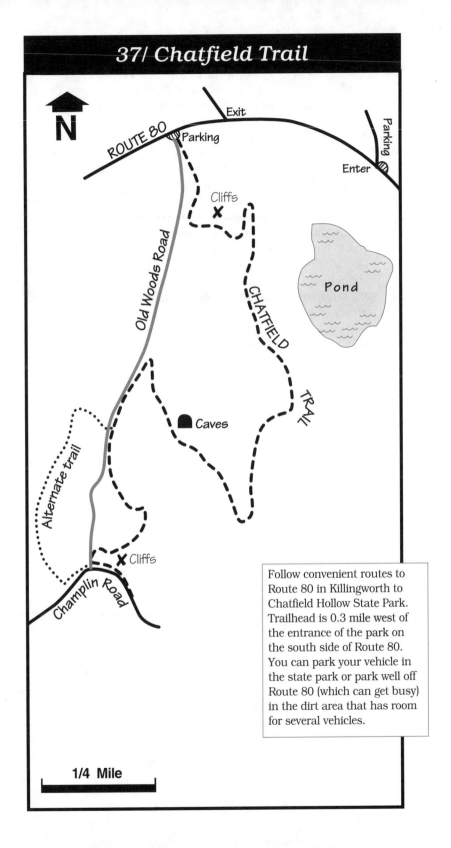

37/ Chatfield Trail

N

ROUTE 80

Exit

Parking

Parking

Enter

Cliffs
✗

Old Woods Road

Pond

CHATFIELD

TRAIL

Caves

Alternate trail

Cliffs
✗

Champlin Road

Follow convenient routes to
Route 80 in Killingworth to
Chatfield Hollow State Park.
Trailhead is 0.3 mile west of
the entrance of the park on
the south side of Route 80.
You can park your vehicle in
the state park or park well off
Route 80 (which can get busy)
in the dirt area that has room
for several vehicles.

1/4 Mile

There is no visible difference between a toadstool and a mushroom. Both names mean the same thing: a fungus that propagates from a spore instead of a seed, has a common root system of fine threads, and subsists upon dead and living organic matter. One of the chief characteristics of both is the absence of chlorophyll.

Many of the more than 3,000 varieties of wild mushrooms growing in the Western Hemisphere are found along the blue-blazed trails of Connecticut. Some of the common species are puffball; beefsteak; olavaria, a member of the coral fungus group; jack o'lantern, the underside of which glows at night; and sulphur or chicken, which when fried is a gourmet's delight but is unpopular with conservationists because it often kills the tree on which it grows.

The common mushroom sold in the markets is the meadow mushroom. Oddly enough its closest look-alike is the most deadly of all known poisonous mushrooms, the destroying angel or fly amanita.

There are many rules and hints about how to detect the poisonous from the edible mushrooms, but there are also too many exceptions. So until you become an expert in fungiology, continue to have fun by admiring rather than devouring these pop-ups of nature.

38

Chatfield Hollow State Park
Killingworth

Distance: 18 miles of hiking trails, shorter loops

Difficulty: Easy, most paved

While the adventure seekers in your family are exploring the Chatfield Trail, those with young children or those who just want to take it easy can explore Chatfield Hollow State Park and its trails.

Located 1.5 miles west of Killingworth center on the north side of Route 80, Chatfield Hollow State Park boasts 356 acres of woodland, 18 miles of well-marked hiking trails, and 7-acre Schreeder Pond. Created in the early 1930s, when the Civilian Conservation Corps (CCC) dammed Chatfield Hollow Brook, today the pond is a popular summer swimming spot (lifeguards are usually on duty) and a favorite of anglers. No boats are allowed on the pond, but land-bound anglers have a chance at sunfish, bullheads, bass, and pickerel. A wheelchair-accessible fishing pier is also available.

In season, you can drive into the park. In autumn the main access road to the park is gated and access then is on foot; leave your vehicle in the large parking lots located near Route 80. Follow the main road in. At your left is a jumbled mass of boulders and interesting rock crevices, evidence of shelters once used by Native Americans who hunted and fished here. The trail to the top is easy to follow and leads to rocks, openings, and an outlook across the wooded valley.

> **TRAIL TIPS**
>
> Outhouses and picnic areas are located in the park. Admission is charged from Memorial Day through Labor Day. Nearby Killingworth has places for purchasing food.

You can then pick and choose what other well-marked trails to explore. One (short) trail leads to replicas of a covered bridge and waterwheel, evidence of earlier industries including grist milling and iron smelting. Other (longer) trails explore the hardwood forests. Birding enthusiasts will want to keep an eye out for Baltimore orioles, phoebes, red-tailed and harrier hawks among other species.

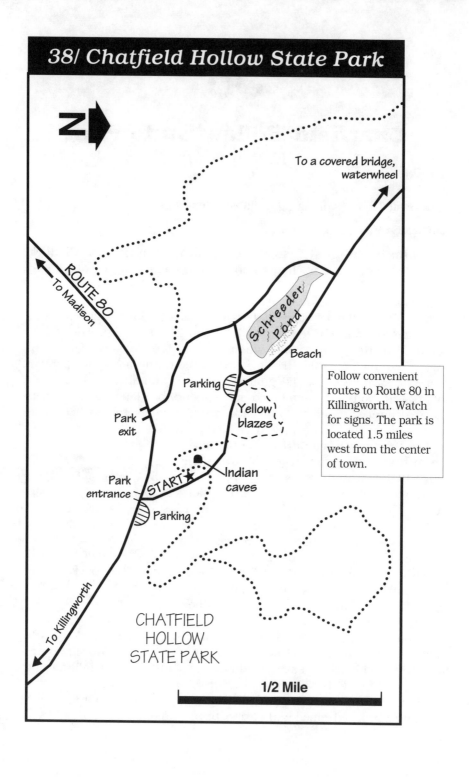

N

To a covered bridge, waterwheel

ROUTE 80
To Madison

Schreeder Pond

Beach

Parking

Yellow blazes

Park exit

Park entrance

START

Indian caves

Parking

To Killingworth

Follow convenient routes to Route 80 in Killingworth. Watch for signs. The park is located 1.5 miles west from the center of town.

CHATFIELD HOLLOW STATE PARK

1/2 Mile

39

Bear Hill Loop

Middletown

Distance: 4.2 miles round-trip

Difficulty: Moderate

This loop walk is on the Eastern division of the Mattabesett Trail, between Route 154 and the Connecticut River. It's a scenic stretch with a high spot, nicknamed the Summit, and a big ledge called the Chinese Wall.

To gain access to the trail, park your car at one of the dirt pull-offs along Brooks Road. Follow the blue-blazed hiking trail south, crossing Bear Hill Road and to the summit of Bear Hill. At 2.25 miles is the Summit, with views to the east. Head back to the main trail as it continues south and passes over the Chinese Wall, providing scenic overlooks of the Connecticut River south from late fall to early spring. The main trail extends for approximately another 2 miles and ends off Aircraft Road for a total loop of almost 4.2 miles.

TRAIL TIPS

No facilities are available. Parking is along the road in several small, well-worn pull-offs. Trails show signs of being crossed by dirt bike paths; stay alert for their passage. Refreshments and food can be purchased in Middletown.

Note

This segment of the Mattabesett Trail is made up of a main trail and several loops. The main trail (more strenuous) is indicated by blue-blazed rectangles; the connecting loop trails (easier) are marked with circular blue blazes. Take care to note the blazes and keep to the trail to avoid being sidetracked.

Portions of the trail wind through mountain laurel "slicks," forest-like areas of this pretty shrub. The curvy laurel branches intertwine to form a dense thicket overhead; the trail passes through areas quite unlike a more typical Connecticut forest of oak, pine, and maple that has only a dash of laurel in the undergrowth.

Smooth outcroppings of twisted and "cooked" (metamorphic/igneous) bedrock can be seen underfoot on the section of the trail that

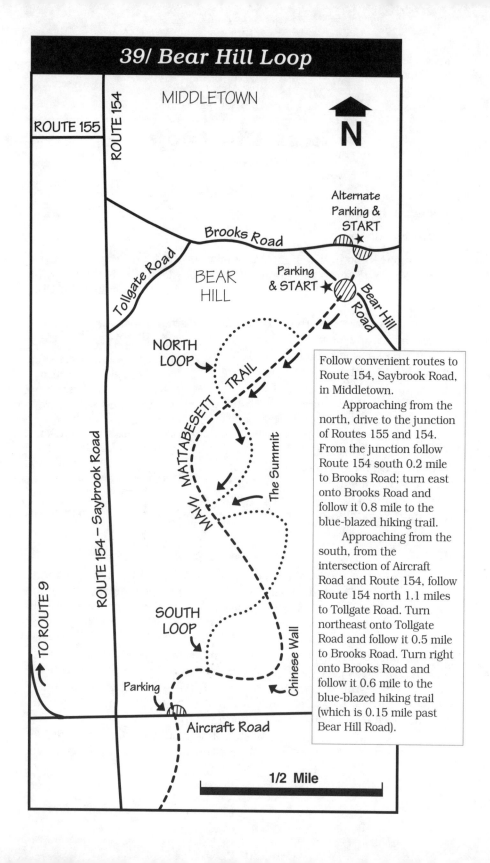

39/ Bear Hill Loop

ROUTE 155

ROUTE 154

MIDDLETOWN

N

Alternate
Parking &
START ★

Brooks Road

Parking
& START ★

Tollgate Road

BEAR
HILL

Bear Hill Road

NORTH
LOOP

MATTABESETT TRAIL

MAIN

The Summit

ROUTE 154 – Saybrook Road

SOUTH
LOOP

Chinese Wall

TO ROUTE 9

Parking

Aircraft Road

1/2 Mile

Follow convenient routes to Route 154, Saybrook Road, in Middletown.

Approaching from the north, drive to the junction of Routes 155 and 154. From the junction follow Route 154 south 0.2 mile to Brooks Road; turn east onto Brooks Road and follow it 0.8 mile to the blue-blazed hiking trail.

Approaching from the south, from the intersection of Aircraft Road and Route 154, follow Route 154 north 1.1 miles to Tollgate Road. Turn northeast onto Tollgate Road and follow it 0.5 mile to Brooks Road. Turn right onto Brooks Road and follow it 0.6 mile to the blue-blazed hiking trail (which is 0.15 mile past Bear Hill Road).

passes under the power lines and, for a short time, through a meadow. Look for shining, mirrorlike mica—an odd mineral that can be peeled off in paper-thin layers. Also found here are such minerals as feldspar and schist. Glassy, almost-clear quartz can be found as well. A simple guidebook on rocks or minerals can add to your enjoyment of this walk.

40

Reservoir Loop
Middletown

Distance: 3 miles

Difficulty: Easy

This pleasant, easy trail offers a little bit of everything: great views, varied environments, even an old quarry. The trail starts on the north side of Brooks Road opposite Bear Hill Road. Follow the trail, a section of the Mattabesett, as it skirts a swamp. At 0.25 mile, the trail swings left across an old woods road. At 0.5 mile (Old Burn Crossing) it intersects with a blue-blazed loop trail; stay straight. A small, abandoned quarry is on your right. Continue on the trail as it crosses a brook and starts a steep climb up around a ledge. Keep to the left of the trail down the back side of the ledge. Rock overhangs dominate here. At 1.2 miles, the trail intersects with Reservoir Road (dirt); continue straight. At about 0.85 mile, you'll cross a brook and begin another steep climb. The summit affords views of two nearby reservoirs.

Once you've taken in the views, continue until 1.35 miles when you come to Rockpile Cave on your left. At this point, take a sharp right and follow the trail along the base of the ledge. Reach the woods road and cross it to go uphill again. Keep an eye out for views of rock formations and the swamp on your right at about 1.95 miles. A little further the trail recrosses Reservoir Road. You can turn right and walk down Reservoir Road for 0.2 mile to the trail on the left, which will take you back to the start.

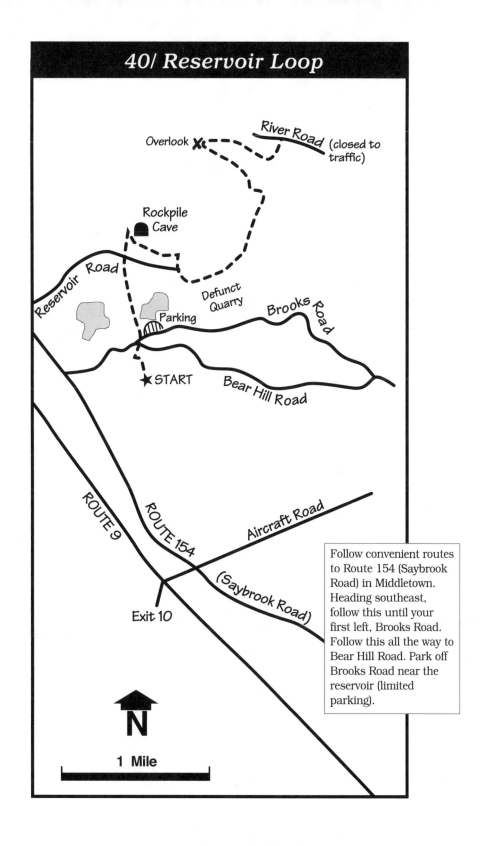

40/ Reservoir Loop

Overlook

River Road (closed to traffic)

Rockpile Cave

Reservoir Road

Defunct Quarry

Brooks Road

Parking

START

Bear Hill Road

ROUTE 9

ROUTE 154

Aircraft Road

(Saybrook Road)

Exit 10

N

1 Mile

Follow convenient routes to Route 154 (Saybrook Road) in Middletown. Heading southeast, follow this until your first left, Brooks Road. Follow this all the way to Bear Hill Road. Park off Brooks Road near the reservoir (limited parking).

41

Bluff Head
Guilford

Distance: 2 miles round-trip on orange-dot trail; 3.8 miles one way hike-through

Difficulty: Moderate to strenuous depending on trail chosen

For a heady and breathtaking climb, Bluff Head on the Mattabesett Trail in the town of Guilford is a sure thing. A path a mountain goat would love takes you to the very brink of a dizzying view that encompasses Hartford to the north and Long Island Sound to the south; Rhode Island can be glimpsed on a clear day. In the summer it's a cool walk under beech, oak, and maple trees—unlike many other traprock ridges, this trail winds along rock that faces east.

Choose one of two routes up to Bluff Head. The blue-blazed hiking trail makes a nearly vertical hike from the very start and presents a stiff climb. In the short distance of 500 feet, the trail rises 190 feet in height. Although the beginning of the trail is unusually precipitous, it is so for only a short distance. After about 550 feet the trail incline lessens and the ascent is easier. This trail continues all the way through to Route 17 in Durham, where you have the option of parking a second car for a through hike.

Choose the orange-dot trail, on the left, for a less steep route that rejoins the main trail on the ridge. The orange-dot trail crosses land held by the Guilford Land Conservation Trust. A steady rain of acorns can be heard at harvest time in late summer.

TRAIL TIPS

No facilities available. Parking is in a dirt lot, which can get crowded. Durham and Guilford offer many places for a trail lunch or after-walk meal.

This is not a trail to walk in rain or icy conditions.

Be properly prepared for this walk with suitable shoes; do not try to negotiate the steep ascent with slippery leather soles. The trail can be treacherous, particularly when coming down.

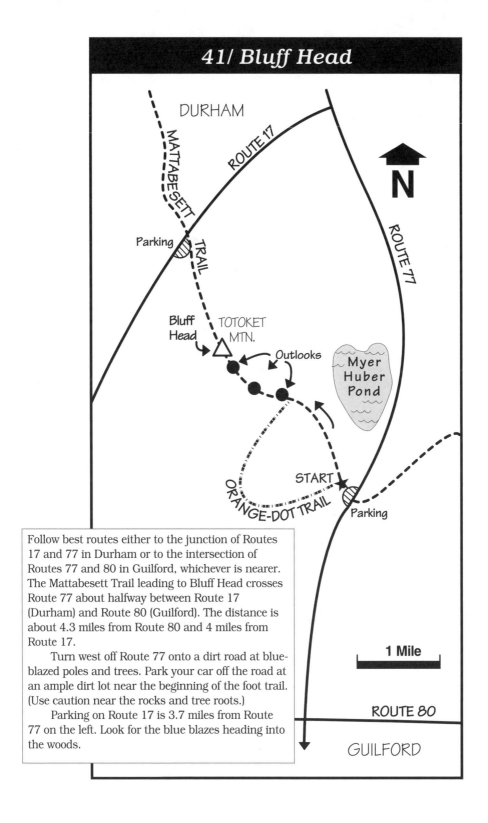

DURHAM

ROUTE 17

MATTABESETT TRAIL

Parking

N

ROUTE 77

Bluff Head

TOTOKET MTN.

Outlooks

Myer Huber Pond

START

ORANGE-DOT TRAIL

Parking

Follow best routes either to the junction of Routes 17 and 77 in Durham or to the intersection of Routes 77 and 80 in Guilford, whichever is nearer. The Mattabesett Trail leading to Bluff Head crosses Route 77 about halfway between Route 17 (Durham) and Route 80 (Guilford). The distance is about 4.3 miles from Route 80 and 4 miles from Route 17.

Turn west off Route 77 onto a dirt road at blue-blazed poles and trees. Park your car off the road at an ample dirt lot near the beginning of the foot trail. (Use caution near the rocks and tree roots.)

Parking on Route 17 is 3.7 miles from Route 77 on the left. Look for the blue blazes heading into the woods.

1 Mile

ROUTE 80

GUILFORD

ORANGE-DOT LOOP

If you didn't want to climb to the summit today, you can follow the orange-dot alternate trail and then loop back to the start on the blue-blazed Mattabesett for a nice 0.8-mile jaunt.

As the path winds steadily upward, you soon find yourself near the edge of a steep cliff, the first of three outlooks.

At the top of the first rise on the right (east), the cliff makes a sheer fall of several hundred feet to the road below. The second outlook provides a look at heart-shaped Myer Huber Pond, 500 feet below.

Bluff Head is the third lookout and requires an almost vertical hike up loose rock and dirt—use care as this is a steep climb very near a vertical drop. This portion of the trail is not for young children, though families can hike the orange-dot trail to the first two views quite easily.

Bluff Head is 720 feet above sea level. The views from the top edge of its cliffs are as awesome as any scene in the state. Long Island Sound far to the south; the fields, distant hills, and the cityscape of Hartford to the north—all invite more than a second look.

Bluff Head is a delightful place to spend an hour or a day. Take a lunch and enjoy it while viewing the far-flung scenes from any of the interesting overlooks on the trail. It is advisable to carry your own water or other liquids for drinking.

Columbine, asters, goldenrod, harebells, as well as hickory, oak, beech, and maple trees can be enjoyed along the route in season. Autumn provides a spectacular display from this lookout.

Once you're ready, leave the edge of the bluff where the trail changes course from north to west and crosses a brook and a high plateau. From here, the blue-blazed hiking trail heads in a general northwesterly direction across Totoket Mountain and down to Route 17 (alternate parking), intersecting it 3.7 miles from Route 77. Note that you'll have to walk along paved Stagecoach Road for about 0.2 mile then turn right onto 17 back to your car.

If you're retracing your steps back to Route 77, choose the orange-dot trail for a walk through the woods or use care while descending the blue trail on the last few hundred feet of the trail from Bluff Head; the sliding, slippery shale can cause severe spills. The round-trip to Bluff Head on the orange-dot trail is about 2 miles.

Hanging Hills
Meriden

Distance: 1 mile from West Peak Road to Castle Craig; 1.2 miles from Castle Craig to West Peak, 1.7 miles on road; all one way

Difficulty: Moderate to strenuous

The blue-blazed Metacomet Trail passes over the peaks of the Hanging Hills of Meriden. The peaks are in Meriden's Hubbard Park and can be reached by car when the park roads are open to vehicles (10:00 A.M. to 4:30 P.M. weather permitting; closed in winter). West Peak, with an elevation of 1,024 feet, offers one of the finest views in Connecticut. East Peak is not quite as high at 976 feet but is home to Castle Craig, a lookout tower up which you may climb for absolutely spectacular views of central Connecticut to Long Island Sound (depending on weather conditions).

The famed landmark "sleeping giant" of Sleeping Giant State Park (see Walk 45) can also be seen quite clearly to the south—try to pick out his head, torso, and legs. Many mountains surround the city of Meriden; looking north it is possible to see the Oz-like towers of Hartford on the horizon.

There are numerous places to begin a walk to these peaks. You can even walk, bike, or drive up Percival Park Road, park, and do the short jaunts to the peaks themselves. This road is about a 3-mile route from the entrance.

To reach the West Peak walks, follow the park road (Reservoir Avenue) along the east bank of Merimere Reservoir to a concrete bridge at its north end. Here, go left on Percival Park Road, then veer right onto West Peak Drive where Perci-val Park Road goes left to Castle Craig.

Note: The road to West Peak is usually blocked even when the park roads are officially open. What you can do is park at the Castle Craig parking area,

To reach the starting point for this walk, follow road map routes (I–691, exit 4, works well) to Hubbard Park, on West Main Street in Meriden. Turn north into the park entrance just west of Mirror Lake. Follow the one-way park road, which encircles Mirror Lake and picnic areas to a stop sign. Proceed straight past a swimming pool on your right to reach the access road (on your left) to the tower. Note that vehicles must return to the entrance gate for the tower access road by 4:30 P.M. when the fencing is promptly locked. (The park remains ungated and open.)

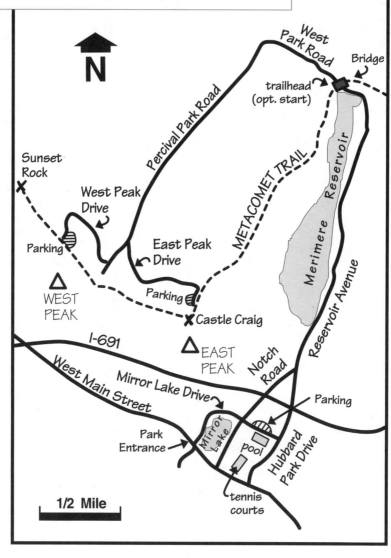

and walk the road (about 1 mile) to West Peak.

Next to the entrance to the West Peak parking area, at utility pole #6775 on West Peak Drive, the blue-blazed hiking trail enters the woods and heads past a power station at the start of the trail. The main trail follows an interior course with side trails leading to outlook points. About 0.6 mile from West Peak, the trail reaches Sunset Rock with its exceptional western view.

From here you can return to the parking lot, walk to its opposite end, and follow an unmarked but obvious trail that offers more wonderful views from West Peak.

A 1.2-mile section of the Metacomet Trail connects East and West Peaks. You can follow this from West Peak to East Peak and Castle Craig if you'd like.

To reach East Peak walks, enter the park and follow Mirror Lake Drive around Mirror Lake to your first left, just as the main road curves to the east. Park near a trail map board and take the white-blazed trail over a walker's bridge that spans I–691 to trails that will lead you up the mountain. Use extreme caution on paths as much of the walk is over loose stone and rubble. The views of the cliffs and narrow gorges are stupendous. There are numerous ledges and small rock shelters hidden in the cliffs. Again, you can follow the Metacomet Trail to West Peak from the summit of East Peak if you'd like.

If you'd like to go straight to Castle Craig, follow the one-way park road from the park entrance past a swimming pool on your right and along the entire eastern length of Merimere Reservoir to a concrete bridge at its north end. The bridge is 1.7 miles from West Main Street. Turn left (west), cross the bridge, and follow Percival Park Road.

The first signs of the blue hiking trail are to be seen here on the bridge and trees on the north side of the road. The blue-blazed Metacomet Trail follows the road for 0.2 mile from the bridge, at which point it leaves the road and leads south along the west bank of the reservoir through the woods approximately 1 mile to East Peak, Castle Craig, and then another 1.2 miles to West Peak. You'll have to park your car in a safe, out-of-the-way spot and walk to the trailhead.

Geologically Speaking

Note the pock-marked stone underfoot—a remnant of the ancient volcanic action that created the Hanging Hills of Meriden. Most of these cliffs are composed of traprock, created when great flows of lava oozed out of long cracks in the floor of the Connecticut Valley. Three major lava flows covered the valley floor. Each one cooled and hardened into traprock and was gradually covered by sand and mud eroded from the surrounding hills.

After the volcanic activity stopped, the whole region was fractured and tilted to the east. Since then, erosion has eaten away at the bedrock.

Thousands of feet of brownstone have been washed to the sea, but the dense, hard, volcanic traprock eroded much more slowly, leaving layers as long ridge lines standing far above the surrounding landscape.

(Excerpted/edited from Conn. Natural Heritage Program Brochure)

You Take the High Road . . .

If the distances are a bit much for you to cover as a round-trip, use the two-car method—leave one car at the foot of the path near the reservoir and the other at the summit's parking lot. Hike from the lower road to the castle, then drive back to the end.

43

Roaring Brook Falls
Cheshire

Distance: 1.4 miles one way, 1.9 miles on hike-through

Difficulty: Moderate to strenuous, some difficult terrain

Roaring Brook Falls is in the town of Cheshire, on the northern portion of the Quinnipiac Trail. Take the blue-blazed trail from Bethany Mountain Road (Route 42) to the north. The trail ascends from the road to a rise of 130 feet, or to an elevation of 720 feet above sea level. There are occasional lookouts along this area. At this point the trail follows the boundary line between Cheshire and water company land. It continues north, passing a quiet pond, skirting a boundary of private property (a horse pasture/house), and traveling over several high ridges with occasional lookouts presenting views to the northeast of Hanging Hills in Meriden (Walk 42). The trail reaches Roaring Brook Falls 1.4 miles from Route 42.

You have several options here: Stop to rest and picnic before you retrace your steps back to your car; go right and down a gorge to the second highest waterfall in the state (on Cheshire Land Trust property); or head off to the left on a trail that leads 0.5 mile to Roaring Brook Road in Prospect (alternative parking or a spot for another car). The Quinnipiac Trail itself goes off to the right just above the main falls, crossing the brook and heading 2.8 miles to its terminus at Route 68.

> ### TRAIL TIPS
>
> No facilities are available. Parking is off the side of a very busy road; use care while crossing it to get to the start of the walk. Note: Hunting is allowed in state forests but not on Sunday; wear blaze orange when appropriate. Nearby Cheshire is a good stop for food and refreshments.

> ### IN THE AREA
>
> The Farmington Canal Greenway, a good side trip, is nearby; follow Route 42/Bethany Mountain Road east, back to Cheshire.

Caution

This section of the Quinnipiac Trail is a short run of difficult footing—

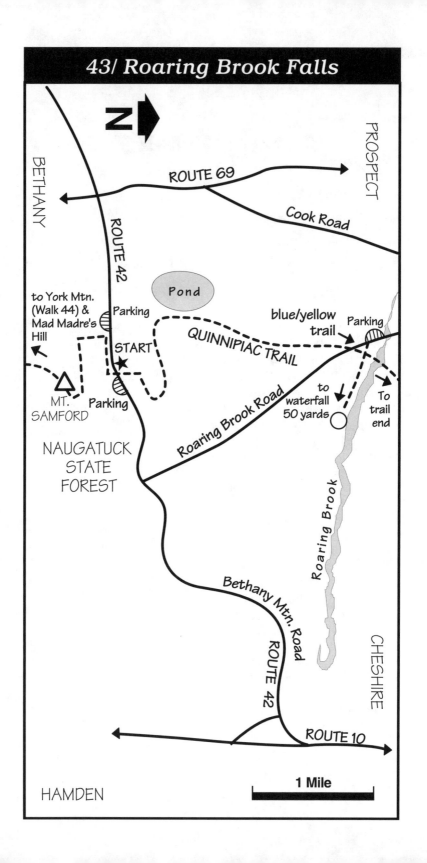

43/ Roaring Brook Falls

N

BETHANY

PROSPECT

ROUTE 69

Cook Road

ROUTE 42

Pond

to York Mtn.
(Walk 44) &
Mad Madre's
Hill

Parking

blue/yellow
trail

Parking

START

QUINNIPIAC TRAIL

MT.
SAMFORD

Parking

to
waterfall
50 yards

To
trail
end

Roaring Brook Road

NAUGATUCK
STATE
FOREST

Roaring Brook

Bethany Mtn. Road

ROUTE 42

CHESHIRE

ROUTE 10

1 Mile

HAMDEN

a jumble of rubble and tumbled boulders on a hillside that should be negotiated with care and proper shoes. The best shoe to wear is ankle-high, with leather uppers and thick composition soles; leather soles are apt to become slippery, especially downhill on leaves.

Map Directions: Take convenient routes to Route 42, an east–west highway between Cheshire and Bethany. From Route 10 in Cheshire, follow Route 42 west for 2.8 miles to where the blue trail crosses; or from Route 69 in Bethany drive east on Route 42 to where the trail crosses the road, 1.2 miles. The crossing is indicated by blue blazes, which are easier to see when traveling east on Route 42, since the trail uses a short stretch of the route before reentering the woods. Park your car off the traveled portion of the highway. Use care; the road can get busy.

To park a second car on Roaring Brook Road in Prospect, follow Cook Road north from Route 69. Turn right onto Roaring Brook Road. Trail head access is on left.

York Mountain

Hamden

Distance: 1 to 1.5 miles round-trip

Difficulty: Moderate to strenuous, depending on route

TRAIL TIPS

No facilities are available. Parking is off the road. Use care navigating the stony trail—seeping water on slick rock can make it slippery in spots.

Wonderful views alone make this hike worth the time! After parking your car on Paradise Road, follow the blazes back along the road past houses then to the Quinnipiac Trail (across from utility pole 7278) that leaves the road at a right angle, west, crosses an old stone wall, and then ascends the east face of York Mountain.

This mountain offers some of the finest panoramic views in the state. Its crest reaches 680 feet high. To take advantage of an extensive bare rock area where one has unobstructed views of the south and the west, the trail follows the south rim of the mountain about 20 feet below its peak. This outcropping of rock makes the ideal place to rest and lunch.

The top of York Mountain is about 1.5 miles round-trip from the start. Should you wish to extend your walk, you may follow the main

ALTERNATIVE ROUTE

The summit of York Mountain can also be reached by parking at Nolan Road and ascending the blue-blazed hiking trail to the top. From here, the hike is steep, but only about 1 mile long one way.

trail west to its junction with the Regicides Trail. This is an easy walk, but keep a sharp eye out for trail markers, which are painted on rocks and downed trees in this area. Watch for a sign (about 10 feet off the ground) that indicates the junction of trails and which way they go.

Hawk Watch

York Mountain is a good outpost from which to observe a natural annual phenomenon—the hawk migration that funnels thousands of these hunting birds through the state in September. Although nature is not always predictable, chances are good that you will see at least a

44/ York Mountain

N

ROUTE 10

HAMDEN

To reach the start of this walk, follow convenient routes to Route 10 in Hamden. Take this route to West Woods Road (just north of the sign for Sleeping Giant State Park at Mount Carmel Avenue). Go west 1 mile on West Woods to Shepard Avenue; go south on Shepard past Nolan Road (alternative start and parking, across from the Hamden Public Works Garage). Continue to follow Shepard to a traffic light. Turn right onto West Shepard for 0.2 mile, then onto Laura Road for 0.3 mile, and turn right onto Paradise Road, a dead end. Park your car off the road.

Rocky Top Road

Road

H.P.W.
Garage

Shepard   Avenue   Light

West Woods

Nolan Road

Old Coach Highway

★

Alternate
START
& Parking

West Shepard Avenue

Shepard Brook

Laura Road

Parking   Paradise Road

QUINNIPIAC TRAIL   ★ START

YORK
MOUNTAIN △
Elev. 680'

REGICIDES
TRAIL

1/2 Mile

few hawks from early autumn through October. With luck and under optimum conditions, it's probable to see many of these magnificent birds as they wing their way south along invisible (to humans) highways. Birds sometimes just spiral along on thermals (the sun-warmed air from rock exposures).

At Lighthouse Point in New Haven, some 20,000 hawks are counted each year during their migration south. For details on hawk watches and migrations, call the Connecticut Audubon Center at Fairfield (203) 259–6305. —*C.B.*

45

Sleeping Giant
Hamden

Distance: Varies with the trail chosen

Difficulty: Varies with the trail chosen

Climb a chin, walk the elbow, or trek up the head of the giant him-self—hikers are sure to feel like Lilliputians while exploring the Sleep-ing Giant, a forested 2-mile traprock ridge that resembles a human figure lying on his back (with his feet to the east and his head to the west). This formation is the centerpiece of Sleeping Giant State Park.

The park is situated mostly in Hamden and includes about 1,400 acres and more than 30 miles of trails, including an interpretive na-ture trail. All trails are indicated by a particular blaze, either by a color or a round, square, triangular, or diamond-shaped marker. The Nature Trail is indicated by painted green circles with a dark pine tree in the center or by green circles with study-station numbers.

The Nature Trail offers an easy, basic education in many things: geology, biology, botany, ecology. The numbered trees and rocks be-side the trail are matched with the numbered paragraphs in the guide: trees, ferns, glacial plains, erosion, the difference between traprock and sandstone, and much more.

The entire Nature Trail loop is about 1.5 miles in length. The first part on the south is easy, level walking and is suitable for all ages and abilities. The last part of the trail (toward the northwest), after the turn near the giant white pine tree, is rougher and steeper. Some may wish to return to start from here. Completing its route, the Nature Trail crosses the paved Tower Trail. You can take the

TRAIL TIPS

Facilities in the park include outhouses, picnic areas, and shelters. More detailed trail maps are available at the map board at the entrance to the park. It's advisable to bring along a map as the many trails crisscross and can be confusing, although all are marked. Also available here (except when supplies run out) are free park map folders and copies of the free booklet, "Self-Guiding Nature Trail in Sleeping Giant State Park," which is published by the Sleeping Giant Association.

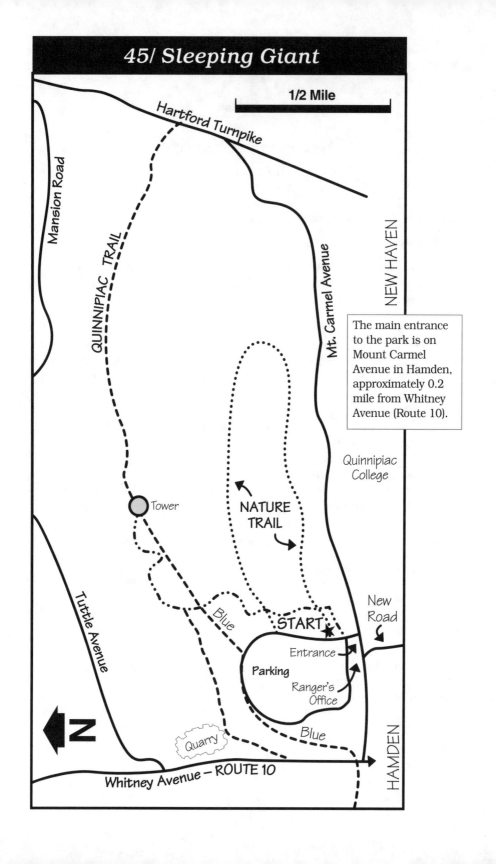

45/ Sleeping Giant

1/2 Mile

Hartford Turnpike

Mansion Road

QUINNIPIAC TRAIL

Mt. Carmel Avenue

NEW HAVEN

The main entrance to the park is on Mount Carmel Avenue in Hamden, approximately 0.2 mile from Whitney Avenue (Route 10).

Quinnipiac College

Tower

NATURE TRAIL

Tuttle Avenue

Blue

New Road

START

Entrance

Parking

Ranger's Office

N

Quarry

Blue

HAMDEN

Whitney Avenue – ROUTE 10

Tower Trail back to your car, or continue on the Nature Trail, which at this point follows orange blazes and descends steeply to the parking area.

For a more strenuous hike, take the blue trail from the parking area. It takes you up and around rocks, dropping down to the trail and leading to a quiet walk beside a stream before going uphill to walk over the "elbow." This path leads up a steep trail that flirts with the very edge of a quarry that once threatened the existence of the Giant's head. The approximately 5.1-mile walk is not a trail for the faint of heart or young children. The view of the steep cliffs where excavations once took place, however, is worth the climb. After reaching the top of the head, traverse the Giant's chest and pick a crossover trail that leads back.

Trails are rated for difficulty; the tower trail and the blue trail are the only two that lead to the stone tower on the Giant's left hip.

More About the Giant

The Sleeping Giant Park Association (SGPA) sponsors guided group hikes year-round. This is a good way to get familiar with some of the Giant's lesser-known paths and local lore. If a walk piques your interest, the association has published a book, *Born Among These Hills* by Nancy Davis Sachse. It can be ordered from SGPA, Box 14, 555 New Road, Hamden, CT 06518.

It's Said . . .

When English colonists arrived in the area in the 1630s, Quinnipiac Indians were living and hunting on the ridge. It's said that the Quinnipiacs venerated the giant, called Hobbomock. He was reportedly a mischievous spirit who fell into a deep sleep after he tore up and diverted the course of the Connecticut River at Middletown. Today he sleeps on, and his woodsy contours are enjoyed by hikers, picnickers, and nature lovers.

46

Southford Falls
Southbury

Distance: Varies with trail chosen

Difficulty: Easy to moderate, some steep climbs, tricky terrain

A great walk through yet another gorgeous Connecticut state park.

Most of Southford Falls State Park's 120 acres lie in the township of Oxford, but the entrance is in Southbury. Eight Mile Brook is the boundary line between these two towns in the area of the park. What looks at first like a roadside picnic area is deceiving—the park is extensive.

Enter the parking area, leave your car, and prepare to explore the many features of the park on foot. The park trails, worn and obvious, may be followed easily with moderate attention and observation.

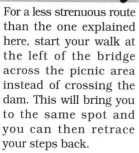

TRAIL TIPS

For a less strenuous route than the one explained here, start your walk at the left of the bridge across the picnic area instead of crossing the dam. This will bring you to the same spot and you can then retrace your steps back.

Picnic areas and outhouses are available at the park.

The most popular walk is to cross the dam at the south end of Papermill Pond to the east bank of Eight Mile Brook, as it falls and cascades swiftly down the deep, rocky ravine. Continue on the path close to the stream (this part can be a little tricky; use care especially with little ones) to the southwest corner of the state park's property. Most of the trails are suitable for all ages and abilities, but some of the areas are steep and will require extra effort and frequent rest stops. If you want to avoid the tough parts, retrace your steps from here. If you're up to it, continue on to visit the lookout tower (worth the visit). The tower is showing its age and requires care when ascending its steps. The top is sturdy, but again, be careful and hold on to those little ones. Once you've taken in the views, loop back to the start. The walk back is easier than the steep one you took up.

A Historical Perspective

In the days of water power, Southford Falls, with its constant and

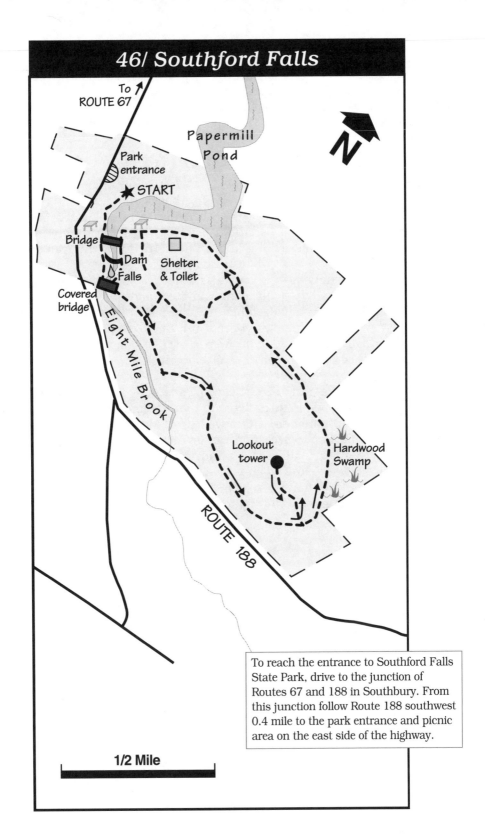

46/ Southford Falls

To ROUTE 67

Papermill Pond

Park entrance

★ START

Bridge

Dam
Falls

Shelter & Toilet

Covered bridge

Eight Mile Brook

ROUTE 188

Lookout tower

Hardwood Swamp

To reach the entrance to Southford Falls State Park, drive to the junction of Routes 67 and 188 in Southbury. From this junction follow Route 188 southwest 0.4 mile to the park entrance and picnic area on the east side of the highway.

1/2 Mile

powerful flow, was the site of several important mills. Water once provided the necessary muscle to turn the wheels of Connecticut's commerce. Perhaps the most successful of all mills at this site was the Diamond Match Company, which recycled old paper and rags to make matchbooks and matchboxes. This once-booming mill was destroyed by fire in 1923.

The Friction Match: A Pocket of Fire

Early in the nineteenth century, one of the world's most important inventions was conceived. In its way and for that period, it was a great step forward, an advance perhaps as beneficial to mankind as the electric switch was in the twentieth century. This world-shaking achievement was the perfecting and manufacturing of the friction match.

The friction match—also known as the lucifer, locofoco, kitchen, wood, or sulphur match—made flint and steel and other crude fire starters obsolete. No animals other than human beings have ever been able to control and maintain fire. Until the invention of the friction match, methods of igniting fire were slow and cumbersome. People therefore tried to keep their fires or embers glowing, quite often a difficult and frustrating task.

In 1834 Thomas Sanford of Beacon Falls perfected the friction match, which was soon in such demand that Sanford found it necessary to increase production. He moved to Bladen Brook in Woodbridge and built a waterwheel that was too big for the brook to turn. Every penny Sanford had in the world went into the folly of that mammoth waterwheel, and when it failed he was so discouraged that he offered to sell his match "recipe" for $10. The Diamond Match Company later bought the formula and made the wooden match a commercial success.

47

Trolley Trail
Branford

Distance: Less than 2 miles with option for more

Difficulty: Easy

A gem of a walk and a paradise for bird watchers, the Stony Creek Trolley Trail between the Pine Orchard and Stony Creek sections of Branford is suitable for all ages and abilities. The entire round-trip is less than 2 miles.

Decades ago, a trolley regularly rattled and clanged along this route. The main trolley station was once located on what is now Stony Creek Green; there was a ticket office and store there, too. Bus service replaced the trolley around 1928, and nowadays the old roadbed is an easy, inviting trail.

The walk offers fine views of salt marshes, tidal creeks, Long Island Sound, and some of the Thimble Islands. This is a site that draws bird lovers, joggers, and cyclists. Egrets and yellowlegs are among the birds that dine in the marshes, and such plants as wild lavender and seaside roses appear in season. You'll also see northern bayberry, shagbark hickory, and oak trees, sassafras, jewelweed, and interesting traprock ledges.

> **TRAIL TIPS**
>
> There are no rest rooms at the trail. Parking is available near the start of the trail. *Caution:* Poison ivy grows abundantly along the pathways.

Youngsters will enjoy crossing the trail's old trestle bridge near Stony Creek. Watch for the small train that travels the spur at the Pine Orchard end, carrying basalt, or traprock, from the Tilcon Connecticut Inc. quarry. (The trainmen usually wave.)

A boardwalk permits you to walk through marsh with dry feet for the entire journey. Benches atop the portion that crosses the tidal river allow visitors to observe the ebb and flow of waters, along with leaping fish. Flocks of small fiddler crabs are especially abundant in the mud flats at low tide where they clack and scuttle away in response to the vibrations of your footfalls. Kingfishers and great blue herons can be sighted, and an osprey platform with nest is located in the marsh.

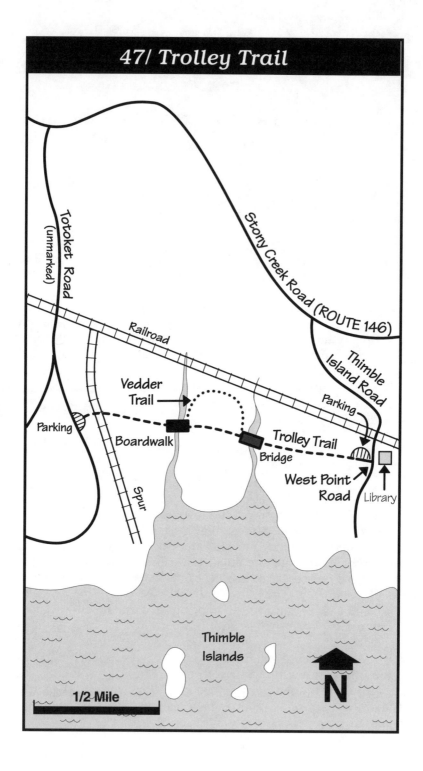

Totoket Road (unmarked)

Stony Creek Road (ROUTE 146)

Thimble Island Road

Railroad

Vedder Trail

Parking

Boardwalk

Spur

Parking

Trolley Trail

Bridge

West Point Road

Library

Thimble Islands

1/2 Mile

N

While the Trolley Trail itself is owned by the town of Branford, nearby Branford Land Trust property includes other trails worth exploring. Farther east there's a white-circle–blazed trail through high granite at the western end of a man-made canyon. This trail makes a loop north of the Trolley Trail to a high granite outcrop with a monument honoring Jennie Vedder (who donated the land) and great views of the marsh and the Thimbles.

IN THE AREA

Great snacks, coffee, ice cream, and sandwiches are available in Stony Creek about 1½ blocks south on Thimble Island Road. (Stony Creek is a very nice village to stroll.)

A Pirate in Connecticut

Capt'n Kidd, or Captain William Kidd, was one of the most colorful scallywags in history (1645–1701). The pirate is reported to have stashed loot up and down the eastern seaboard, and an actual portion of his treasure was recovered from Gardiner's Island, one of the Thimble Islands. (The islands that make up the Thimbles range from lone rocks to those large enough to host a whole community.)

In 1699 Captain Kidd inscribed his initials and those of his wife on a rock on Pot Island; Money Island is so-called because it was believed Kidd hid his treasure there. There is also a Kidd's Island.

Although Kidd was hanged in 1701, the legend goes that he hid half his plundered loot in various locations on the Thimble Islands. (Which other islands he picked out of the hundreds, no one knows— yet.) —C.B.

Map Directions: From I-95, take exit 53. Follow signs to 146 east. Stay on 146 for a total of approximately 4.6 miles (from the off-ramp) as it bears to the left past a church. Route 146 turns right at stop sign and merges into Montowese Street. Continue under a train trestle and over Branford River. At next stop sign take a left onto Indian Neck Avenue. At the fork, take a left onto Sybl Avenue as it travels along Long Island Sound. Stay on this road; it bears right at another fork and passes Pine Orchard Market. Take a left onto Blackstone Avenue (you are now 4 miles from I-95). You'll now pass Young's Park on your left. At 4.6 miles, take a right onto unmarked Totoket Road (it's in the middle of a golf course). Stay on Totoket until you see a driveway marked Tilcon 190 on the left. Turn in and follow the road a short distance to a parking area. Leave your car and cross the tracks to follow the trail. (NO TRESPASSING signs apply to the nearby Tilcon operations, not to any trails.) This is the Pine Orchard end of the trail.

To reach the Stony Creek entrance, stay on Route 146 at golf course and follow it to the left (instead of turning right onto Totoket). Follow it to a fork, where you stay to the right. This is Thimble Island Road. At four-way intersection, turn right. At 0.5 mile, turn onto West Point (you'll see the Willoughby Wallace Memorial Library on your left). Parking is abundant at the end of this road, near a ballfield. Follow the narrow path to cross the trestle bridge to the marshes.

48

Bartlett Arboretum
Stamford

Distance: 5 miles possible; option for more

Difficulty: Easy

A living showcase of trees, shrubs, plants, and flowers, the Bartlett Arboretum of the University of Connecticut at Stamford offers opportunities to explore living bamboo, a collection of "witches' broom" trees, a secluded garden, a collection of nut trees, a bog walk, and several woodland trails—all in addition to educational programs for the public and professionals in horticulture and plant science. A variety of workshops and occasional plant sales are offered as well.

Walkers of all ages and abilities can enjoy the unblazed but well-defined trails that crisscross the mixed-hardwood forest, a red maple swamp, Poorhouse Brook, and a two-acre pond on the sixty-three-acre preserve. One may observe and study the trees, wildlife, and wildflowers. An interesting feature is a sturdy boardwalk winding through the swamp and bog areas—fun in springtime when turtles and frogs are abundant. A perennial garden is sure to inspire any gardener seeking fresh ideas.

It is not necessary to take a guided tour, and any time is a good time to visit. There is something of interest taking place at all times and in every season at the arboretum. The Rose A. Thielens Self-Guided Ecology Walk corresponds to numbered stations along the walks. The booklet is available at the office for $1.00.

The Lowdown

The Bartlett Arboretum is open to the general public, free of charge. (Donations are welcome.) Maps are available in the parking lot gazebo, the visitors' center porch, and from the receptionist (during office hours). A backpack filled with children's activities and games to use on a visit may be checked out here; return it when you leave. A small, but well-stocked shop offers neat things: compasses (under $4.00), books, notecards, gardener's soap, and related items. Portable rest rooms are located by the parking lot gazebo.

48/ Bartlett Aboretum

ROUTE 137

Take convenient routes to the intersection of Merritt Parkway exit 35 and Route 137 (High Ridge Road). From the intersection, drive north on Route 137 for 1.4 miles to Brookdale Road. Turn west onto Brookdale Road and follow it to a road on the right, which is the well-marked entrance drive to the arboretum. Follow signs to the parking area.

Swamp

Boardwalk

WOODLAND

Pond

STAMFORD

Stone Dam

BROOK TRAIL

Poorhouse Brook

BARTLETT ARBORETUM

GAZEBO TRAIL

Brookdale Road

Map Board

Gazebo

Lab

Parking

Parking

CEMETERY TRAIL

Office

Entrance

Visitor Center

Greenhouse

1/2 Mile

N

The History

In 1913 Dr. Francis Bartlett, a dendrologist (we didn't know either—it's someone who is an expert in trees and plants) and founder of the Bartlett Tree Expert Company, acquired the farm as his home and established a school and laboratory for his company. Through the years he assembled a large number of plant specimens from around the world. In 1965 the research lab was moved to North Carolina and the North Stamford property was bought by the state of Connecticut.

IN THE AREA 🌿

The Stamford Nature Center is located nearby. Stamford also has a wealth of places for eating out and trail supplies.

The arboretum staff and members of the Bartlett Arboretum Association are constantly working on and offering varied programs of interest to the novice and expert alike. Various guided tours are offered throughout the year, and numerous education programs are available for schools and larger groups. For information, contact: The Bartlett Arboretum, 151 Brookdale Road, Stamford 06903; (203) 322–6971.

Telling the Season by Plants and Sounds

If any season may be considered superior, it has to be spring. The poet Henry Van Dyke wrote, "The first day of spring is one thing, and the first spring day is another. The difference between them is sometimes as great as a month."

Whether spring is on time or comes a bit late, it is a period of anticipation and fascination. The skunk cabbage pushes up a tentative probe but is careful to keep her cowled hood tightly closed. The red-winged blackbird suddenly announces his arrival, sounding his cheery unmistakable ok-a-lee call while clinging to a swaying upright reed. When the bloodroot and shadbush flaunt their white blossoms and the yellow adder's-tongue cautiously appears, spring is truly here.

49

Putnam Memorial
Redding

Distance: Almost 2 miles entire loop

Difficulty: Easy

This is a fascinating walk through Connecticut's own Valley Forge. Set in a beautiful, historic park, this is a walk for all abilities. Putnam Memorial State Park comprises more than 250 acres and includes one of the best-preserved winter campsites of the Revolutionary War.

The entrance to the park is dominated by a dynamic, larger-than-life bronze statue of General Putnam on his majestic horse, created by sculptor Ann Hyatt Huntington when she was ninety-three years old. The sculpture depicts the general as he made his dramatic mounted escape from pursuing British dragoons, down the one hundred steps carved into the precipice at Horse Neck, Greenwich, 1779.

The main gate is flanked by two high blockhouses guarding the gateway. Enter the gate and stop to pick up a detailed map available just inside the entrance on the right in a wooden box. Ascend to the crest of a hill past an obelisk made of native granite, crowned by a huge cannonball. The monument was erected as a memorial to the men who served here and faced such harsh conditions.

The memorial shaft is at the beginning of the actual encampment, which is studded with mound after mound of rock piles. These are the fallen chimneys and walls—or firebacks—left where they tumbled from soldier's huts. There is much of historic interest here, including a reconstructed guardhouse, the 12-by-16-foot log hut that housed twelve men, an officer's hut, Phillip's Cave, a cemetery, and a powder magazine.

TRAIL TIPS

Picnic areas and outhouses are located in the portion of the park near Lake Putnam (not the historic portion). Bring along refreshments; there are no concessions available. The park gate is locked at 5:00 P.M. Parking is then limited to the spaces near the entrance outside the gate.

A visit to the museum is a must. It is built on the site of the original picket post from which sentries observed the comings and goings of the area. Inside the museum is a display of items uncovered on an

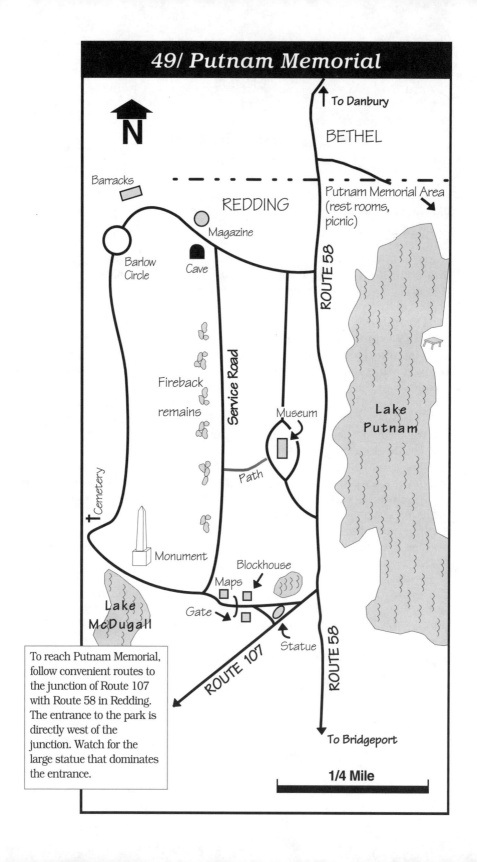

N

To Danbury

BETHEL

Barracks

REDDING

Putnam Memorial Area (rest rooms, picnic)

Magazine

ROUTE 58

Barlow Circle

Cave

Fireback remains

Service Road

Museum

Lake Putnam

Path

Cemetery

Monument

Blockhouse

Maps

Gate

Lake McDugall

Statue

ROUTE 107

ROUTE 58

To Bridgeport

To reach Putnam Memorial, follow convenient routes to the junction of Route 107 with Route 58 in Redding. The entrance to the park is directly west of the junction. Watch for the large statue that dominates the entrance.

1/4 Mile

archaeological excavation—including a portion of a pipestem, buttons, and a lock. A collection of wooden tools is also of interest.

You may drive the service roads to get a quick overall view; then park your car and wander on foot to the various points of interest. You may observe an ongoing excavation that will continue to add information about the encampment.

A Historical Perspective

The Putnam Memorial State Park in Redding memorializes the site of the winter encampment of the right wing of the Continental Army during the Revolutionary War. In this area 8,000 to 9,000 troops suffered through the stormy winter of 1778 to 1779. General Washington's encampment during the previous winter at Valley Forge may have received more publicity, but the hardships endured by the men of the Redding encampment were equally severe.

Israel Putnam was the senior major general of the Continental Army at the time of the encampment at Redding. Affectionately called "Old Put" by his men, it was he who persuaded army leaders that the base at Redding was a logical and strategic military position. (Meet up with "Old Put" again on Walk 18, Mashamoquet Brook State Park, for another episode in the life of this remarkable man.)

The fight for independence was on. The British were entrenched in New York and continued to harass the colonists in Connecticut. The previous year the soldiers of King George III had attacked and burned Danbury, a major supply depot for the army. From the Redding encampment, Old Put contended, his men could defend the heart of Connecticut and help protect the southeastern coast of the state, the western area, and be prepared to return to the Hudson River in the event of an attack.

Sherwood Island

Westport

Distance: Less than 1 mile with option for more

Difficulty: Easy

Explore the Westwood Nature Trail or just wander at a leisurely pace along a 1.5-mile-long beach on Long Island Sound at Connecticut's first state park, Sherwood Island.

If you'd rather walk with a purpose than meander aimlessly, start at the far eastern end of the park's beach. Continue west on the beach to a fence at the western edge of the park. Turn right, leaving the beach, to enter a picnic grove on higher ground. The grove rises a few feet above the surrounding marsh; this higher area provides a vantage point and observation post for bird-watchers. When conditions are favorable and with proper footgear, the marsh may be investigated with care.

After the walk head to the roof deck of the pavilion for a panoramic view of the park grounds, Long Island Sound, and on a clear day, New York City. Should the weather be too blustery to picnic comfortably at an outside table, there is a protective glass screen on the pavilion's lower level. This mammoth picture window provides a pleasant outlook to the sound and also affords unexpected warmth when the sun shines through it.

A small boardwalk leads into the nature walk area from the east parking lot. Amtrak trains pass nearby, and the roar of Interstate 95 traffic can be heard at the park marshes. This walk is suitable for all ages.

A Historical Perspective

The area was used in season by Native Americans, and early settlers arrived in 1648, following the end of the Pequot War. Legend has it that Captain Kidd, the notorious pirate, used the island as a rendezvous point.

The park was named in honor of the Sherwood family, early settlers here who migrated from England's Sherwood Forest, legendary home to Robin Hood and his band of followers.

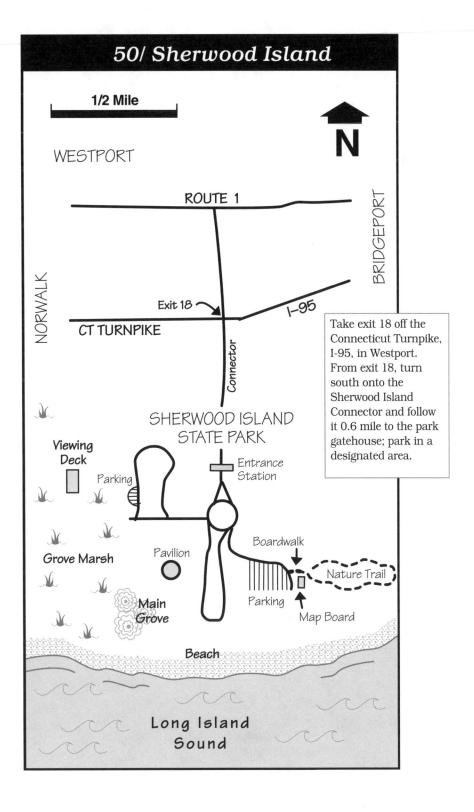

50/ Sherwood Island

1/2 Mile

N

WESTPORT

ROUTE 1

BRIDGEPORT

NORWALK

Exit 18

I-95

CT TURNPIKE

Connector

SHERWOOD ISLAND STATE PARK

Viewing Deck

Parking

Entrance Station

Take exit 18 off the Connecticut Turnpike, I-95, in Westport. From exit 18, turn south onto the Sherwood Island Connector and follow it 0.6 mile to the park gatehouse; park in a designated area.

Boardwalk

Nature Trail

Grove Marsh

Pavilion

Parking

Map Board

Main Grove

Beach

Long Island Sound

Today, Sherwood Island State Park is the only shoreline state park in Fairfield County. Established in 1914 it boasts 234 acres of sandy beach, marshes, groves of linden and maple trees, picnic facilities, and a spacious modern pavilion. The park's major feature is the 1.5-mile-long sweeping beach, bounded by Long Island Sound to the south.

Squantz Pond
New Fairfield

Distance: 2 miles with option for more

Difficulty: Easy to moderate depending on route

This is a wonderful walk through beautiful Pootatuck State Forest. The hiking trails start from the west side of the parking area. The main trail starts at the north end of the picnic area and follows the edge of the pond's western shoreline. Trails and side paths are not blazed but are so worn and well-defined as to make them easy to follow. Keeping close to the water's edge, go north to the first of four major streams, splashing down several hundred feet from the mountain above to the pond (more of a lake in appearance) below. Crossing the stream, follow the main path along the water's edge, always bearing right.

There are many side trails along the route to explore. You needn't worry about getting lost: The pond is always visible, and you have only to walk toward the water to pick up the main trail that parallels the shoreline.

Before investigating any side trails, it would be advisable to stay on the main path past two other streams, the last of which is about 1.5 miles from the picnic area. From the third stream the trail is less trodden but nevertheless visible and easy to follow to a small peninsula with an unobstructed view of the entire waters. This spot is about 2 miles from the start and is an ideal place to rest before returning to your vehicle.

The trail is strewn with huge boulders, tumbled helter-skelter from the high and massive rocky ridge that rises almost directly from the pond's edge to a height of more than 400 feet. A loop trail to Council Rock is worthy of an afternoon expedition, or choose a more strenuous route to Lookout Point. Depending on the amount of time and energy you have to spend, explore the streams and side trails, where numerous caves can be found.

> **TRAIL TIPS**
>
> Dogs are not allowed May 1 to September 30 in the park area. An entrance fee is charged until the end of September. Trail food or after-trail meals are available in nearby towns.

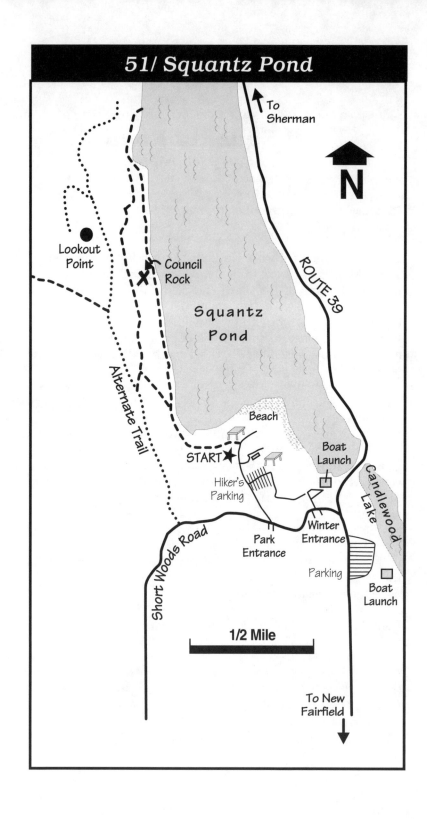

51/ Squantz Pond

To Sherman

N

ROUTE 39

Lookout
Point

Council
Rock

Squantz
Pond

Alternate Trail

Beach

Boat
Launch

START

Hiker's
Parking

Candlewood
Lake

Short Woods Road

Park
Entrance

Winter
Entrance

Parking

Boat
Launch

1/2 Mile

To New
Fairfield

Area Overview

Squantz Pond is an arm of the beautiful Candlewood Lake, the largest body of water within Connecticut. The lake was created in 1928 by the Connecticut Light and Power Company's hydroelectric dam, built on Rocky River in New Milford. The lake covers ten square miles and has 72 miles of shoreline. Marinas abound in the area.

Around the same time that Connecticut Light and Power's dam was being built, the state acquired the park, originally a 172-acre farm. The park's roads and hiking trails were developed by the Civilian Conservation Corps (CCC) in the 1930s.

In the warm months, the park offers a bathhouse, concession stand, sandy beaches for children, deeper waters for stronger swimmers, scuba diving (Let us know if the watering trough is still there!), fishing, boating, water skiing, picnicking, or just relaxing. In the colder weather, you can hunt, hike, and snowmobile the adjoining Pootatuck Forest, which boasts 1,000 acres.

A Historical Perspective

The park is named for Chief Squantz, sachem of the Pootatuck Indians. The tribe frequented this land for hunting and fishing and held powwows with nearby tribes on a ledge called Council Rock. Candlewood Lake is so-called because Indians made torches from the resinous pine that grew here.

In the early 1700s, Squantz agreed to sell his land to early settlers from Fairfield. But after the men returned home to draw up the agreement, things changed. The sachem had passed away, leaving his sons in charge of the tribe. They refused to sell the land to the settlers for about four years, then relented and made a profit of sixty-five English pounds. Many Indian artifacts have reportedly been found amid the rugged hills that surround the park, including an "Indian war canoe," at the bottom of Squantz Pond. Excited archaeologists prepared to extricate the "canoe" from its watery hole when a local resident inquired "as to why his father's old watering trough should be considered such a strange and wonderful creation."

Map Directions: The entrance to Squantz Pond State Park is off Route 39 in New Fairfield. Approaching from the south at the intersection of Routes 37 and 39 in New Fairfield, turn north onto Route 39 and follow it 3.8 miles to the entrance. From the north, at the junction of Routes 37 and 39 in Sherman, take Route 39 south approximately 6 miles to the park entrance west of the highway. Watch carefully for signs.

Enter the gate and park in one of the designated areas. The first lot you'll pass is for boaters only. Park in the next one.

52

River Road
Kent

Distance: 5 miles one way

Difficulty: Easy to moderate

This is a level, pleasant riverside walk on a section of the Appalachian Trail (AT) that offers quiet water to explore in summer; varied environments that provide homes to all sorts of wildflowers, birds, insects, and small mammals; and spectacular foliage in autumn months. This walk is suitable for all abilities. Of all the AT's 53 miles in Connecticut, most of them are through steep and rugged terrain. However, there are a few sections of this trail that are more or less level and relatively easy to walk. This walk is one of those sections.

It covers a 5-mile stretch along the west bank of the Housatonic River between St. John's Ledges in Kent and Silver Hill in Sharon. When the trail reaches Silver Hill, it goes up the hill, then descends sharply. Along the walk you will see numerous streams tumbling down the face of the mountain range and flowing into the Housatonic River. The river and the mountain streams along this portion of the Appalachian Trail have an eye-appeal unmatched by sights from higher elevations. The trail is shaded and wide with oceans of ferns, bee balm, and wildflowers. Massive trees line the banks. During the summer crayfish scuttle among the river-smoothed rocks. Tracks of deer and the tiny imprints of their accompanying fawns, alongside blue heron tracks (they resemble dinosaur prints), and the hand-like prints of raccoons dot the many sandbars. A cloud of butterflies can be glimpsed as it takes to the air from a resting spot along a quiet river cove. Be sure to tuck in a pair of shoes (thick-soled sandals) for wading into the river.

> **TRAIL TIPS**
>
> An outhouse is located near the start of the trail. The river is popular for fishing and summer outings. The village of Kent has several family-style restaurants and an ice cream/sandwich shop. Sections of this trail are on or close to state forest land and private land open to hunting. Hikers should wear blaze orange and be aware of deer season (check dates in autumn).

Drive to the intersection of Routes 7 and 341 in the center of Kent. From the intersection follow Route 341 west across the Housatonic River Bridge to Skiff Mountain Road. It is the first road to the right, west of the river. Turn north onto Skiff Mountain Road and follow it 1.1 miles to the junction with River Road. Skiff Mountain Road bears left here. Follow River Road to its end, where the foot trail that is a section of the Appalachian Trail begins.

Park your car in the small grassy lot, and follow the white-blazed Appalachian Trail north as it parallels the wide, easy-flowing Housatonic River. Trail and road cling close to the river on the east. The parking area is at the end of River Road, about a mile past St. John's Ledge, where River Road ends.

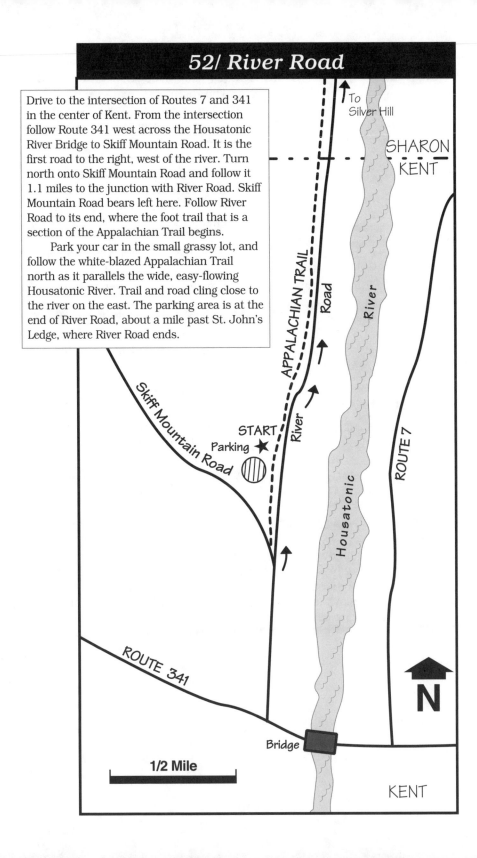

To Silver Hill

SHARON
KENT

APPALACHIAN TRAIL

River Road

River

START
Parking

Skiff Mountain Road

Housatonic River

ROUTE 7

ROUTE 341

N

Bridge

1/2 Mile

KENT

Birdlife is abundant; Canada geese and mallards share the river with hikers and sunbathers. The distinctive clattering call of the belted kingfisher can be heard. This area has been named one of the ten best birding spots in Connecticut. Some of the sightings have included the saw-whet owl, cerulean warbler, black vulture, golden-winged warbler, and yellow-throated warbler. In autumn the sky and blazing foliage on the mountains reflected in the river water are stunning.

Alert: Wet, icy, or snowy conditions, however, can make it very difficult to follow this trail, and heavy rains or spring snow melts can turn the river into fast-moving water, so watch the weather before you set out.

You may walk the entire distance or shorten your walk to whatever length you wish. Trail maps are available from a small wooden box attached to a towering sycamore tree at the end of River Road. (You'll have to walk to this point as only foot traffic is allowed to this point.)

A Bit of History

The AT is 2,150 miles long and passes through fourteen states. Work on the national scenic trail started in 1921 and was completed in 1937.

The Connecticut section of the Appalachian Trail is maintained by volunteers from the Connecticut chapter of the Appalachian Mountain Club. While out on the trail, consider that it is possible (should you wish) to keep walking this path north to Maine, or turn around and tramp southward all the way to Georgia. The trails committee that helps maintain this section of the AT asks that hikers observe a few simple rules: Carry out what you carry in; fires are allowed in the designated areas only; use the facilities/bathrooms available on the trail. This section of the AT sees heavy use as a recreational area; help the volunteers keep it in good shape.

53

Cobble Mountain
Kent

Distance: Almost 3 miles round-trip

Difficulty: Strenuous

Be forewarned that this challenging walk through Macedonia Brook State Park in the town of Kent is not suitable for very young children or the fainthearted. It involves scrambling over rocks and around boulders and tramping uphill using switchbacks. This is a tough trail, but once you get to the summit, you'll be glad you took the challenge.

After parking your car, follow the white-blazed loop trail northwest toward Cobble Mountain, which at 1,380 feet, is the highest point in the area. From its starting point, the trail soon joins old Civilian Conservation Corps (CCC) road (dirt and grass), once called Sharon Road. Follow this road for about 0.3 mile then turn right for another 0.3 mile then turn left on Cobble Mountain Trail ascending steeply for 0.75 mile to Macedonia Ridge Trail. Follow blue blazes toward the summit of Cobble Mountain. Once near the top, follow the blue-blazed trail west (right) to the crest of Cobble Mountain. The view from here is extensive and magnificent. It is one of the finest outlooks in the state with views of multiple ridges and mountain ranges. New York State is visible to the west on a clear day.

When you've had enough of the view, follow the blue-blazed trail 0.3 mile to the juncture with the green-blazed Pine Hill Trail, which descends south another 0.3 mile to CCC road, head south on this road 0.4 mile to the starting point.

Alert: The blue-blazed hiking trail comes down from the mountain over rough and rugged terrain. Although the hazardous portion of this trail is short, it should be negotiated with care. It is advisable not to try this section when it is wet or covered with snow. Under these conditions

TRAIL TIPS

For an unforgettable experience, time your visit for sunset and watch the sun dip behind the mountain crests with the clouds aglow. Remember, if you do this bring a powerful flashlight (with working batteries!) for your not-so-easy trip back down the mountain.

Food and refreshments can be purchased in the village of Kent, located nearby.

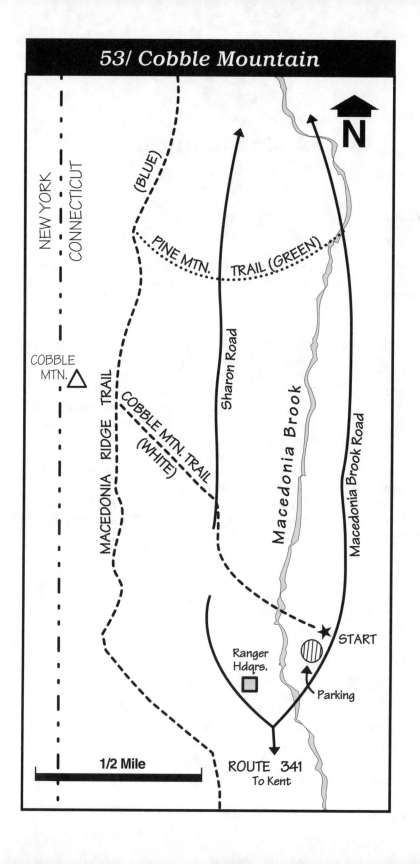

N

NEW YORK

CONNECTICUT

(BLUE)

PINE MTN.   TRAIL (GREEN)

COBBLE
MTN.

MACEDONIA RIDGE TRAIL

COBBLE MTN. TRAIL
(WHITE)

Sharon Road

Macedonia Brook

Macedonia Brook Road

Ranger
Hdqrs.

START

Parking

ROUTE   341
To Kent

1/2 Mile

do not try the green-blazed trail, either. It would be better to retrace the white-blazed trail back to your car, and even this route is best avoided under adverse weather conditions.

An Area Overview

Macedonia Brook State Park, composed of 2,294 acres, has an abundance of all those things that appeal to naturalists. Whether your interest is geology, botany, wildlife, hiking, or just a desire for quiet and solitude, you may satisfy it here. The park has a variety of trails, from easy strolls suitable for families with young children to quite strenuous and rugged hikes. There are several loop trails of varying lengths that bring you back to the starting point without retracing your steps.

Macedonia Brook flows through 4 miles of picturesque gorge in the heart of the park in Nodine Hollow. The main road passes through the park from Route 341 on the south to the Sharon-Kent boundary line on the north. All but one of the trails start from the main park road. Those to the east are generally less steep than those to the west.

Each trail is blazed with its own color: white, red, yellow, blue, green, or orange. A map showing the various trails and other features may be obtained from the ranger on duty. In season the picnic and campsite areas in the park are very popular. For those who wish to get away from the crowds, winter is the ideal season to visit. Outhouses are available in the park year-round.

Indian Pipes

Along the Cobble Mountain Trail look for the ghostly white Indian pipes, a plant that resembles ceremonial peace pipes used by Native Americans. Indian pipes are approximately 3 inches tall and usually grow in a cluster. They are fragile, but after maturing they turn black, tough, and dry; the dried form can be seen year-round. The plant, also called ice plant or corpse plant, grows in rich, shaded woods, never in open sunlight. —C.B.

Map Directions: Macedonia Brook State Park's south entrance may be reached from the intersection of Routes 7 and 341 at the center of Kent. From this intersection drive northwest on Route 341 approximately 1.7 miles to Macedonia Brook Road, which is the main road through the park. Turn north onto this road and follow it to the park entrance, indicated by the sign. About 1 mile from the entrance, the log cabin ranger headquarters is located between Macedonia Brook Road and the old Civilian Conservation Corps (CCC) road, once called Sharon Road, on the left (west).

The white-blazed trail begins on Macedonia Brook Road. It is marked by a sign saying COBBLE MOUNTAIN where it crosses a footbridge, near the pavilion just north of the ranger headquarters. After parking your car in the lot, follow the white-blazed trail northwest.

54

Ratlum Mountain
New Hartford

Distance: 7 miles round-trip with shorter options available

Difficulty: Easy to moderate; it is not too difficult going uphill if you take your time.

This walk along the Tunxis Trail begins near the midpoint of Ratlum Road, which begins in New Hartford and ends in Barkhamsted. Follow the blue blazes from Ratlum Road as the trail winds north, passing a pasture with barbed wire fencing on your right, ascending gradually and easily to the top of Ratlum Mountain, less than 1 mile from the starting point. Be sure to sign in at the trail register, placed in a wooden box mounted on a tree at the top.

From the summit, when trees are bare, there are outstanding views of the valley to the north, Lake McDonough, the Compensating and Barkhamsted reservoirs, and the east branch of the Farmington River. The rest of the year, the leaves obscure the views. In the winter you can see skiers riding up the lifts and zooming down the slopes of Ski Sundown.

The trail continues north from Mount Ratlum 2.5 miles to the Barkhamsted terminus of Ratlum Road. Wild turkeys are frequently spotted along this stretch. The round-trip from one Ratlum terminus to the other is approximately 7 miles. You may do all of it or return from any point along the trail.

Map Directions: Approaching from the south and west, follow the most convenient route to the intersection of Routes 44 and 219 in New Hartford. From the intersection follow Route 219 east 1.5 miles to Ratlum Road in the township of New Hartford.

Approaching from the east, drive south to the junction of Route 179 with Route 219 in Barkhamsted. From the junction follow Route 219 southwest 1.5 miles to the north end of Ratlum Road, in the township of Barkhamsted; continue on Route 219 for 3.75 miles to the south end of Ratlum Road, in New Hartford.

Turn northeast onto Ratlum Road, passing slopes of Ski Sundown and following blue blazes on trees along the road until the blazed trail enters the woods. Park your car and follow the blazed trail north.

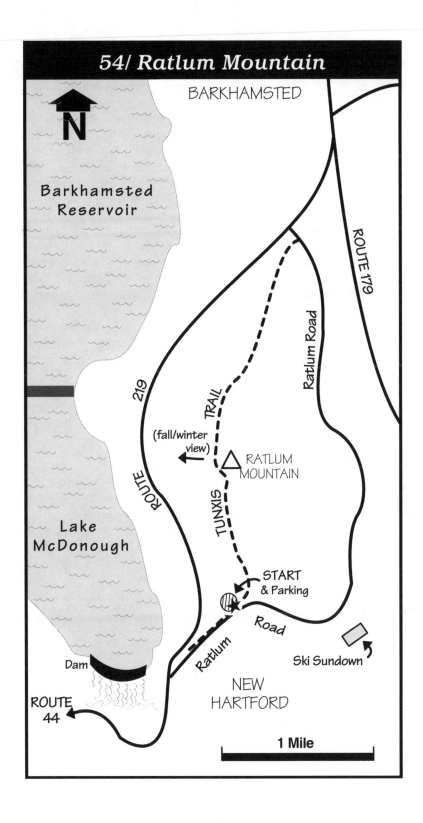

BARKHAMSTED

N

Barkhamsted
Reservoir

ROUTE 179

Ratlum Road

219

TRAIL

ROUTE

(fall/winter view)

△ RATLUM
MOUNTAIN

TUNXIS

Lake
McDonough

START
& Parking

Road

Dam

Ratlum

Ski Sundown

ROUTE
44

NEW
HARTFORD

1 Mile

A Natural Interest

IN THE AREA

Nearby Collinsville is a worthy day trip with a coffee shop–bookstore, a kayak and canoe center, and quiet streets for strolling. This is a good place to go after the hike.

When walking the woodland trails during any season except winter, it is probable that you will see one or more bumblebees. You can call them either bumble or humble bees, but bumble is more common. Both names suggest the humming, buzzing, droning sound made by these insects when in flight. The scientific name of the genus is *Bombus,* Latin for buzzing or humming.

The bumblebee has a large black body covered with a thick fuzzy coat of white or yellow hair. Its flight is not so graceful as that of the honeybee, yet it maneuvers expertly in flight. After examining a bumblebee a scientist once declared that aerodynamically, due to its large body, clumsy design, and small wing surface, it should never be able to fly. Fortunately for us, the bumblebee does not know the rules and miraculously she does fly.

We owe much to the bumblebee for her services as a pollinator of plants. Those flowers with deep corollas, which cannot be reached by the short-tongued honeybee, must be served by the longer-tongued bumblebee.

The bumblebee is a social insect, but unlike honeybees, the bumblebee colony does not live over winter; only the young pregnant queens survive, coming out of hibernation in the spring to start a new colony.

Winter Hiking

Winter is one of the best seasons for hiking—there are no insects, it is easier to dress comfortably for cold weather than hot, there is no foliage to block views, and snow tracks tell interesting stories.

To most animals, snow may prove to be both an asset and a liability. The quality and quantity of a snowfall may be the difference between life and death for predator and prey. A light crust on deep snow may help a small animal escape from a floundering pursuer. A snow-covered pile of brush offers animals shelter from the cold and safety from predators.

Just something to think about while you're in their territory.

55

Bear Mountain
Salisbury

Distance: 12 plus miles round-trip

Difficulty: Strenuous

Bear Mountain is in the township of Salisbury and may be reached by numerous trails. For our purposes, you'll be following the Appalachian Trail (AT) to the peak of Bear Mountain. This is one of the most challenging and rewarding walks in this book. The day-long, more than 12-mile walk offers the highest scenic outlook in the state.

The blue-blazed Undermountain Trail, a popular access trail to the AT, starts here. Follow the Undermountain Trail—which begins to ascend steadily—for a little more than a mile to the Paradise Lane Trail, also blue-blazed, on the right. Take Paradise to go up a plateau, past a swampy area with ferns and a pond, and across an open ledge to reach the white-blazed AT. Turn left on the AT and soon travel very steep slopes of a ledge.

At the crest of Bear Mountain, you'll find a stone monument, blueberry bushes, and misshapen, wind-beaten trees. Along the entire pathway you'll also find great views from outlooks in all directions—the Catskills to the west, Twin Lakes to the east, towering Mount Everett to the north, and Mohawk Mountain to the southeast.

Continue to follow the white blazes; the rocky path will give way to an old woods road. When you come to the blue-blazed Undermountain Trail on the left, take that to return to the parking lot.

TRAIL TIPS

AT trail maps are available at the beginning of the trail, as is an outhouse. You should be prepared for this walk: Wear boots, carry adequate water, and allow enough time to reach the summit and return before sundown—this is an all-day walk.

IN THE AREA

Salisbury has great treats for the trail or afterward. The Village Store on Main Street has detailed topographical maps, as well as outdoor equipment supplies.

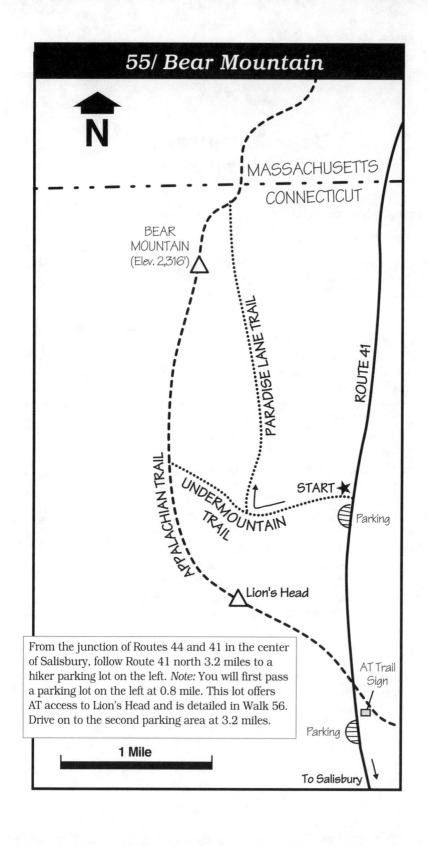

55/ Bear Mountain

N

MASSACHUSETTS
CONNECTICUT

BEAR
MOUNTAIN
(Elev. 2,316')

PARADISE LANE TRAIL

ROUTE 41

UNDERMOUNTAIN TRAIL

START

Parking

APPALACHIAN TRAIL

Lion's Head

From the junction of Routes 44 and 41 in the center of Salisbury, follow Route 41 north 3.2 miles to a hiker parking lot on the left. *Note:* You will first pass a parking lot on the left at 0.8 mile. This lot offers AT access to Lion's Head and is detailed in Walk 56. Drive on to the second parking area at 3.2 miles.

AT Trail
Sign

Parking

1 Mile

To Salisbury

The Bear

Bear Mountain attracts hundreds of hikers to its crest, which is 2,316 feet above sea level. It is the highest mountain peak entirely within the bounds of the state, but oddly enough, it is not the highest point in the state. Connecticut's highest elevation of 2,380 feet is on the Connecticut–Massachusetts boundary line as it passes over the south shoulder of Mount Frissel, the peak of which is in Massachusetts. Bear Mountain is the highest scenic outlook, however, where you may see a virtual ocean of mountain peaks rippling off to the horizon.

56

Lion's Head

Salisbury

Distance: 4 miles round-trip

Difficulty: Strenuous

This walk should be planned as an all-day excursion. A challenging walk, it rewards you with incredible views of the Berkshires, quiet woods, massive trees, and outcrops of garnet-studded rock.

Access to the white-blazed AT trail is gained by following the blue-blazed access trail, which ascends gradually, passing through forest with some stupendously large trees. Natural steps of tree roots and stones are underfoot, and white birch, many with multiple trunks, are abundant. Glades of maple accent the quiet woods.

TRAIL TIPS

This is rugged country; wear sturdy boots and carry adequate water. An outhouse is located near the AT parking lot, 0.8 mile from the junction of Routes 44 and 41. AT trail maps are available at the start of the walk from the map board.

Near the top is a rock staircase and junction of trails; continue right on the white-blazed AT to the top of Lion's Head. This involves a steep climb up a rock knob. Trails marked blue and white run together, divide, and then combine again atop the mountain. From the summit is a view of endless mountains, the Berkshire Hills, and a view of Connecticut, Massachusetts, and New York.

To the right and left of the trail are outlooks. Twin Lakes can be seen to the east, and Bear Mountain looms ahead to the north.

You can continue the walk north to Bear Mountain or return to your vehicle via the same white-blazed route.

Note: Be sure, when retracing your steps down the mountain, to stay on the white-blazed trail—the same one used in ascending. A short section of a blue-blazed trail continues straight ahead as you descend Lion's Head, but does not intersect with the AT and ends at a small road, far from your parked vehicle!

56/ Lion's Head

To →
Bear Mtn.

APPALACHIAN TRAIL (White blazed)

To Massachusetts

LION'S
△ HEAD

Blue
trail

ROUTE 41

Trail
ends →

Hill Road

Bunker

START
★

Parking

To Salisbury

Take the most convenient route to Route 41 in Salisbury. Leave your vehicle at the hikers' parking lot at 0.8 mile northwest of Salisbury on Route 41. The lot entrance is just after two signs that depict hikers, where the AT crosses the road (the lot for Bear Mountain is farther north on the same road).

1/2 Mile

Connecticut's State Mineral: Garnets

Pieces of garnets glow dark red underfoot as you climb upward, approaching the crest of Lion's Head. The garnet was named Connecticut's state mineral by the General Assembly in 1977. It varies in color from pale to dark tints, usually reddish. The mineral has been used as an abrasive throughout Connecticut's industrial history—for the base of grinding wheels, saws, and garnet paper, a type of sandpaper.—*CB*

Insects

Just one step from our own doorstep, or a few steps farther to the blue-blazed hiking trails of Connecticut, are natural miracles, which will enthrall even the most blasé. The only requirement is that one go afoot slowly, with curiosity and a willingness to patiently watch and wonder. At first one must learn the art of seeing, not just looking.

A few of the most common insects are spiders, ants, wasps, bumblebees, ladybugs, and dragonflies; each has a story to tell. The spider constructing her expertly engineered web; the carpenter ants herding and milking their domesticated cows, the aphids; and the tiny spittlebug hiding safely in her white bubbly foam nest in the grass are all fair game to the observant eye.

Leatherman Cave
Watertown

Distance: 2.6 miles round-trip

Difficulty: Moderate to strenuous

This is a primarily uphill walk over rocky cliffs to one of the caves where the legendary Leatherman is said to have frequently made a stop on his endless travels throughout the state. With scenic outlooks, this section of the Mattatuck Trail in a segment of state forest in Watertown involves climbing and some bare, flat-rock exposures. Use care (especially with children or inexperienced hikers) when near cliff edges and when descending to the cave—it's rocky with very steep drops!

To begin the walk, follow the blue-blazed trail in an easterly direction from where you parked your car. The trail gets steep in some places as it goes up and over large rockfaces glittering with mica, to a 650-foot-high overlook with fine views. Follow the trail to a point where another trail intersects; don't get sidetracked, go straight. You'll come to another intersection where you go left through a small swamp. You then come to a Y; go right after the Y and start an uphill climb. Watch for the blue blazes on rocks as the trail can be washed out and rocky. The crest of the overlook is reached at approximately 1 mile from the starting point where you parked your car. Follow the well-marked trail along the edge of the hill.

The trail dips down from this lookout and then begins the ascent to the top of Crane Lookout. This area was burned in a forest fire about ten years ago, so many of the trees are secondary growth and there is an abundance of birch trees. Keep following the trail for about another 0.5 mile to Crane Lookout, which presents magnificent views in every direction.

Map Directions: Follow road map routes to the intersection of Route 109 with Route 6 in the town of Thomaston. Drive southwest on Route 6 for 1 mile, passing Black Rock State Park at 0.5 mile, to the Mattatuck Trail crossing, indicated by an oval blue-and-white trail sign and by blue-blazed trees. There is limited parking off the road, which can get busy. Park well off the road if you can, and use caution when crossing to the trail.

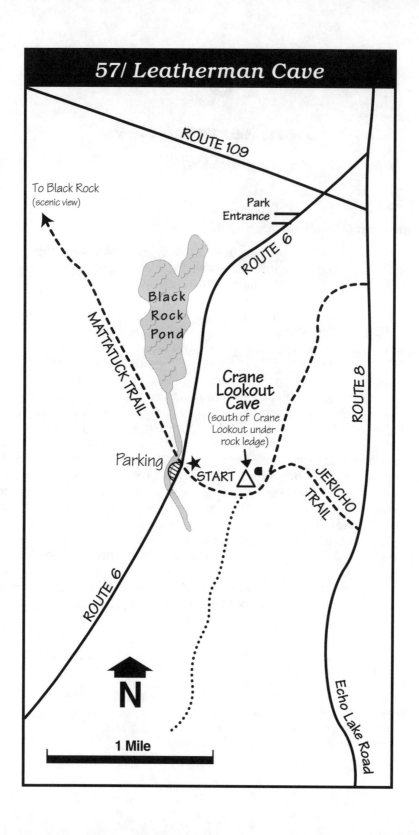

57/ Leatherman Cave

Note the dull red garnets (ranging from dots of color to nuggets) in the rocks underfoot, as well as snowball-like blobs of quartz, ranging in hues from almost pure white to those with an orangeish cast.

As you head down to the base of Crane Lookout, south side, you'll come to two arrows painted on a rock pointing out two trails. The trail to the left leads you to Leatherman Cave, a most unusual and interesting geological formation, which is also known as Rock House. While descending the trail, which is more of a side path off the main blue-blazed hiking trail, note the leathery frills of rock tripe (a type of lichen) that adorn many of the south faces of rock. The trail to the cave is well traveled, but use care as there are some steep drops. Blue blazes lead you through the caves.

Then track back uphill to the blue-blazed hiking trail, and follow it as it dips and climbs onward to its eventual descent to a level forest and meadow area. An unmarked dirt path intersects the Mattatuck Trail before its intersection with Jericho Trail, a side trail leading south to Frost Bridge. You may wish to explore a short distance in this area before returning to your car. The total walk is 2.6 miles round-trip from Route 6.

A Historical Perspective

The Connecticut legend of the Old Leatherman can trace its unlikely roots back to the bankruptcy of a small leather business in France and the resulting broken betrothal.

The man who became known as the Old Leatherman was first reported in Connecticut in 1862. Thereafter he roamed the state in a circuit, always in a clockwise direction, between the Connecticut and Hudson Rivers. It is claimed that he made the trip winter and summer, arriving at the same places every thirty-four days.

Although the Leatherman roamed back and forth across Connecticut for twenty-seven years, very little is known about him. Only near the close of his life were bits of his story learned. His name was Jules Bourglay; he was born near Lyons, France. He worked for his prospective father-in-law, who owned a prosperous leather business. The young man ruined the business by miscalculating the market and was then jilted by his sweetheart. These losses apparently

165

affected him mentally, and he became an eccentric wanderer. He left France and came to America.

He wore leather clothing from head to toe. His hat, coat, vest, trousers, and shoes were made of pieces of hide crudely laced together. It is estimated that his attire weighed more than sixty pounds, not including two large leather bags in which he carried all his other possessions. One anecdote states that he wore these things as a penance and a constant reminder of his misfortunes.

He begged by gestures, never speaking but expressing thanks for food and tobacco with grunts. His overnight stopping place was in one of many caves along his route. He could not be persuaded to sleep in a house or barn. All his sleeping, even his last, was in a cave. He was found dead near Ossining, New York, in a cave.

If all the caves in which the Leatherman is reported to have slept had a sign reading LEATHERMAN SLEPT HERE, these surely would outnumber Washington's sleeping places in Connecticut. An interesting account of his travels and life can be found in *The Romantic Legend of Jules Bourglay: The Old Leatherman,* by Foster Macy Johnson (Bayberry Hill Press). The tale makes for interesting reading before or after the hike, especially to children or those who love local lore.

All that remains of the famous wanderer is a leather mitten and a pouch—both preserved by the Connecticut Historical Society in Hartford. Sadly his jacket and pants, along with the odd ten-pound shoe, acquired by the Eden Museum in New York, were destroyed in a fire.

58

Black Rock
Watertown

Distance: 1.75 to 2.5 miles round-trip depending on route

Difficulty: Strenuous

This is a steady and sometimes strenuous walk up a steep trail to Black Rock ledges and beautiful vistas. Not the easiest walk, this one isn't for everyone.

This walk can be started and finished in two different places. You can start from Route 6 (see Walk 57) and travel about 2.5 miles round-trip; or you can start from within Black Rock State Park and travel about 1.75 miles round-trip along the Mattatuck Trail.

To start your journey to the top from the parking lot within the state park, cross a picturesque trestle bridge that spans the outflow of the pond and a small dam. Bear right after the bridge. (The trail that leads to a campground goes straight ahead from the bridge.) Heading northeast, you'll soon cross a small wooden footbridge (marshy in wet seasons) and see blue blazes. At about 1 mile from the parking lot, a red-blazed trail veers off to the right and provides an alternate (longer) route to the top. Follow the blue-blazed hiking trail and ascend through shaded glades, passing rocky outcrops. It is a sometimes stiff climb uphill over smooth rocks and stepped ledges. Take a break to enjoy the serenity of the woods, then ascend to Black Rock itself, a high spot providing a wonderful view of the valley, the park, and the pond far below.

The distance from the pond to the rock is less than a mile.

> ### TRAIL TIPS
>
> A fee is charged at the park entrance from Memorial Day to Labor Day. Rest rooms and plentiful parking are offered at the park. A detailed trail map is available at the ranger's office. Use care with children near cliff edges at the summit and during steep climbs on the trail. Camping is available at the park or at nearby campgrounds, offering the option of staying over and walking several of the trails in the area.

You may retrace your steps to your starting point or continue ahead, turning right onto a red-marked trail to make a somewhat longer loop back. Alternatively you may continue northward on the blue-blazed

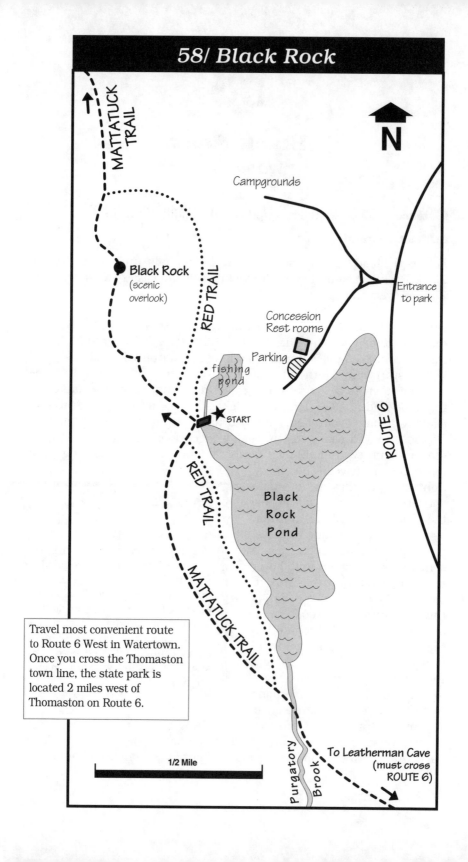

MATTATUCK TRAIL

N

Campgrounds

RED TRAIL

Black Rock
(scenic
overlook)

Entrance
to park

Concession
Rest rooms

Parking

fishing
pond

★ START

ROUTE 6

RED TRAIL

Black
Rock
Pond

MATTATUCK TRAIL

Travel most convenient route
to Route 6 West in Watertown.
Once you cross the Thomaston
town line, the state park is
located 2 miles west of
Thomaston on Route 6.

1/2 Mile

Purgatory Brook

To Leatherman Cave
(must cross
ROUTE 6)

Mattatuck Trail to an abandoned road, less than a mile from Black Rock, that marks the end of the Mattatuck State Forest. You can also follow the trail south into other areas of the forest.

Great stands of evergreen hemlock, along with white birch and ruffle-barked silver birch trees, can be found on this hike. Should you hike during warm weather, a dip in the pond would be a perfect ending to a day at the park.

Park Overview

Black Rock State Park in Watertown has every element of an ideal nature preserve. In the rolling hills of the state's western highlands, it includes a stretch of the Mattatuck Trail, as well as Black Rock Pond, Purgatory Brook, and steep ledges covered with pine, hemlock, and oak. The 439-acre park was given to the people of Connecticut in 1926 through the efforts of a far-sighted citizens' conservation group. As with many other state parks, development of access roads and other facilities came about through the efforts of the many young men involved in the Civilian Conservation Corps (CCC), one of the economic recovery programs during the Great Depression. The CCCers are gone now, but evidence of their hard work remains for all to enjoy.

Today the park offers a seasonal snack bar; sandy, lifeguarded beach; and seasonal bathhouse changing rooms.

A Historical Perspective

It is said that an early user of what are now park trails was King Philip, an Indian chief who pursued colonial farmers in an attempt to discourage them from settling in the area. The stone points and implements of Connecticut's first residents are reportedly still found in the park; look carefully and you might be lucky enough to find some (at least it's fun to look).

Black Rock is not actually "black rock" but a combination of minerals that include quartz and mica. Early settlers in the valley were granted rights by Native Americans around 1657 to mine graphite, a dark-colored rock—hence its name.

59

Peoples State Forest
Pleasant Valley

Distance: 11 plus miles possible

Difficulty: Easy

The Peoples State Forest, located roughly 5 miles north of New Hartford in the Pleasant Valley section of Barkhamsted, is a nature walker's paradise. There are more than 11 miles of hiking trails through 2,954 acres of beautiful woodlands and along the west branch of the Farmington River, designated as a Wild and Scenic River by the National Park Service.

The forest was established in 1924 through the efforts of the Connecticut Forest and Park Association. Assisting the association, citizens' groups, including the Daughters of the American Revolution and the Connecticut Federation of Women's Clubs, bought and donated land to the people of Connecticut for approximately $8.00 an acre.

Color-coded hiking trails were established and named for people who helped develop the forest.

Robert Ross Trail (blue blazes)

This trail begins at the Stone Museum and extends 2.2 miles to the Warner Road turnaround.

After parking, look for the blue-blazed trail passing between a set of posts.

Ascend along the soft bed of an old road grade, touring amid white pine–deciduous woods. At 0.1 mile, find Stone Museum, a small, seasonally open natural history museum. Skirt it, veering left across a gravel parking area to resume the tour.

Pass amid some head-tilting big trees and bear left at the 0.2-mile junction with the orange-blazed Agnes Bowen Trail (the loop's return). Foot trail now continues the tour, ascending amid mixed forest with mountain laurel, maple–leafed viburnum, fern, and sarsaparilla; a few tulip poplars grace the woods.

The blue trail tops out at 0.6 mile; now descend a picturesque laurel corridor. Pass the occasional rock sporting a squirrel's acorn harvest. At 0.8 mile, bear right, following a woods road to the King

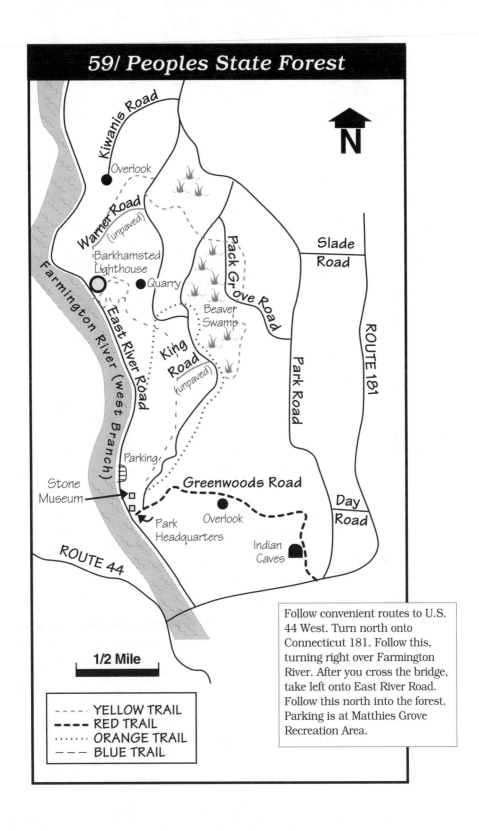

59/ Peoples State Forest

N

Kiwanis Road

Overlook

Warner Road (unpaved)

Slade Road

Pack Grove Road

Barkhamsted Lighthouse

Quarry

Beaver Swamp

Farmington River (west branch)

East River Road

King Road (unpaved)

Park Road

ROUTE 181

Parking

Stone Museum

Greenwoods Road

Overlook

Day Road

Park Headquarters

Indian Caves

ROUTE 44

1/2 Mile

- - - - YELLOW TRAIL
━ ━ ━ RED TRAIL
· · · · · ORANGE TRAIL
– – – BLUE TRAIL

Follow convenient routes to U.S. 44 West. Turn north onto Connecticut 181. Follow this, turning right over Farmington River. After you cross the bridge, take left onto East River Road. Follow this north into the forest. Parking is at Matthies Grove Recreation Area.

Road turnaround; there, angle left into forest. Where the trail forks, bear right, staying with the blue blazes for a similar rolling tour through relaxing woods.

At 1.3 miles, angle uphill, crossing the orange Agnes Bowen Trail again. Now, a defined slope drops away west to the Farmington River. The terrain grows rockier, as the tour passes below an outcrop crest with rounded cliffs and sharp-edged breaks.

Descend steeply for a short distance, meeting the southern branch of the yellow Jessie Gerard Trail (1.65 miles). It descends left, reaching Barkhamsted Lighthouse (the site of Chaugham's cabin); an Indian settlement cemetery, with primitive head and foot stones; and ultimately, East River Road (0.25 mile). Chaugham, a Native American, married the rebellious daughter of an American colonist. At night the light from his cabin shined like a beacon, alerting stagecoach travelers that New Hartford rested but 5 miles off.

For the loop, follow a shared-segment of the Robert Ross/Jessie Gerard Trail (blue and yellow) uphill to the right. At 1.8 miles, meet the northern branch of the Jessie Gerard Trail, which descends 299 stone steps toward Chaugham's cabin; bear left (south) where it forks to view the cellar hole and graves. For the loop, continue climbing. In autumn, skeins of honking geese pass south over the Farmington River.

At 2 miles, the blue trail heads right to Warner Road. For the loop, stay on the yellow Jessie Gerard Trail for a treacherously steep ascent over stone steps and canted outcrops, reaching the first of two overlooks at 2.1 miles. It offers a mostly wild view south out the Farmington Valley. When dressed in fall foliage, the landscape inspires. Top the ridge and hike north through forest to claim Chaugham Lookout (2.4 miles), for a northwestern perspective that overlooks the rural charm of Riverton.

The loop resumes north, still following yellow blazes for a slow descent amid hemlocks. Pass the bookend multiton Veeder Boulders, 2.5 miles. The descent quickens. Soon, bear right on a woods road to reach Greenwoods Road, the main forest artery. Turn right and resume the hike, following the yellow Charles Pack Trail (2.9 miles), as it heads left just beyond Big Spring Recreation Area.

Pass the rock-rimmed circular pool of Big Spring and descend along Beaver Brook, touring rich hemlock-hardwood forest. Despite a rocky forest floor, the trail remains relatively rock-free. Cross a side brook on hewn logs to reach little-used Beaver Brook Road. Go left, cross the brook on the road bridge, and turn right, following blazes through Beaver Brook Recreation Area, a small, rustic picnic site.

Ascend through similar forest upon a less-defined path, now echoing the hemlock slope above it. Proceed over a scenic rock wall and descend to cross Pack Grove Road a second time. Big hemlocks continue to embellish the tour; find more rock walls and foundations. At the fork at 4.65 miles, bear right and descend to cross a footbridge over Beaver Brook.

As the trail ascends, it skirts Beaver Swamp, betrayed only by a change of lighting in the forest. At 4.8 miles, leave the Charles Pack Trail and follow the orange Agnes Bowen Trail left to close the loop.

Enjoy a scenic rolling stroll, once again amid greater concentrations of mountain laurel. Skirt the edge of James Stocking Recreation Area to descend a rocky root-bound foot trail along a drainage. Tulip trees decorate the path. At 5.8 miles, cross the drainage via stones to cross Greenwoods Road. Close the loop at the 0.2-mile junction (5.9 miles) and backtrack the blue Robert Ross Trail to Matthies Grove parking.

The Compost Heap of Life: One Big Cycle

From year to year as we revisit forest areas, it may appear at first glance that nothing has changed. The forest seems to have a calm stability, a harmony, a feeling of something eternal. Yet there is constant change. The forest floor is covered with the litter and debris of fallen plant and animal life that is constantly under attack by such organisms as earthworms, springtails, fungi, and bacteria; these decomposers are in turn preyed upon by larger forms of life.

Every living thing develops from elements that once were a part of other living things. Our own bodies are composed of second-hand materials that may have been active ad infinitum in other forms of life. Some of the atoms and cells in our own makeup may have been functioning in the body of a giant dinosaur that once sloshed around in prehistoric swamps.

WHAT'S SO SPECIAL ABOUT UNSPOILED, NATURAL PLACES?

Beauty   Solitude   Wildness   Freedom   Quiet   Adventure
Serenity   Inspiration   Wonder   Excitement
Relaxation   Challenge

There's a lot to love about our treasured public lands, and the reasons are different for each of us. Whatever your reasons are, the national **Leave No Trace** education program will help you discover special outdoor places, enjoy them, and preserve them—today and for those who follow. By practicing and passing along these simple principles, you can help protect the special places you love from being loved to death.

THE PRINCIPLES OF LEAVE NO TRACE

- Plan ahead and prepare
- Travel and camp on durable surfaces
- Dispose of waste properly
- Leave what you find
- Minimize campfire impacts
- Respect wildlife
- Be considerate of other visitors

Leave No Trace is a national nonprofit organization dedicated to teaching responsible outdoor recreation skills and ethics to everyone who enjoys spending time outdoors.

To learn more or to become a member, please visit us at www.LNT.org or call (800) 332–4100.

Leave No Trace, P.O. Box 997, Boulder, CO 80306